FRIDA
KAHLO

Frida Kahlo Rivera. 1931.

FRIDA KAHLO

MALKA DRUCKER

University of New Mexico Press

Albuquerque

For GSB, with whom I share life and art

Copyright © 1991 by Malka Drucker. All rights reserved. University of
New Mexico Press paperbound edition published 1995 by arrangement
with the author and with Bantam Doubleday Dell Publishing Group Inc.
Second paperbound printing, 1999

Book design by Jaya Dayal.
Cover design by Linda Mae Tratechaud.

Library of Congress Cataloging-in-Publication Data
Drucker, Malka.
Frida Kahlo / Malka Drucker.
p.   cm.
Originally published: New York: Bantam, 1991.
Includes bibliographical references and index.
ISBN 0-8263-1642-5 (pa.)
I. Kahlo, Frida.
2. Women artists—Mexico—Biography.
3. Kahlo, Frida.
I. Title.
N6559.K34D7   1995
759.972—dc20   95-13666
[B]
CIP

Contents

Acknowledgments

I would like to thank the following people for their insights, memories, cooperation, and generosity.

Anne McGovern deserves special thanks for suggesting Frida as a subject. Through interviews with Emmy Lou Packard, Lucienne Bloch, and Arturo Bustos all that I had read about Frida came alive: they helped me to hear her voice. Hayden Herrera's definitive biography of Frida, David and Karen Crommie's film, *The Life and Death of Frida Kahlo*, and Carol Leadenham at the Hoover Institute were particularly helpful resources in my research.

I am also grateful to Ed Marquand, Deborah Bloomfield, and Hayden Herrera for their help in leading me to other Frida devotees. For the right to reproduce works of art in their possession, I would like to thank the public and private owners of the paintings and photographs used in this book. Lucienne Bloch, Marilyn Lubetkin, and Dr. Salomon Grimberg merit special appreciation for their magnanimity and interest in this project.

Key thanks to: Betsy Gould, Beverly Horowitz, and Diana Ajjan for their editorial wisdom, courage, and faith; Barbara Karlin and Janet Zarem for their friendship; my mother, who showed me my first Rivera painting; my sons Ivan and Max for their abundant patience and support; and finally, to Gay, who didn't type the manuscript but did everything else to make this book a joy to write. —MALKA DRUCKER

Foreword

ALTHOUGH Mexico's best-known woman artist, Frida Kahlo, has been dead thirty-five years, her revealing, often pain-filled, self-portraits have provoked intense curiosity about who she really was, even among those who knew her. The legends and myths surrounding Frida's brief, full life add to the intriguing mystery.

To understand this richly complicated woman requires a willingness to read between the lines, because the story of Frida Kahlo is like Frida herself—magnetic, profound, and occasionally shocking. Hardly a model citizen, she drank, smoked, swore, and had many romantic partners, yet one doesn't have to live her life to learn from her.

Instead of allowing her pain to be destructive to herself or others, Frida turned it into art. By painting nightmares as well as dreams, she exposed her sorrows, fears, and struggles. Her work moves us not only because we feel compassion for Frida or share her afflictions, but because it helps us to feel our own grief. She offers a lesson in survival, a life lived without inhibition, and a courageous spirit.

My candle burns at both ends;
  It will not last the night;
But, ah, my foes, and, oh, my friends—
  It gives a lovely light.

EDNA ST. VINCENT MILLAY,
From "First Fig"
A Few Figs from Thistles

CHAPTER 1

My Grandparents, My Parents, and I

LEANING close to the cold windowpane in her bedroom, Frida took a deep breath and exhaled forcefully, forming a frosty circle in the middle of the window darkened by night. Her full black eyebrows met one another as she concentrated on drawing a door that filled the circle. Confined to her bed for months by polio, the only part of Frida that still leapt and played was her inventive mind. She wished she could leave her boredom and step through the door into a fantastic world.

Staring at the translucent entrance, Frida imagined herself walking through it and crossing a large field that led to a dairy called Pinzon; through the *O* in the sign she slid easily into the center of the earth. There Frida found a little girl her same age, six years old, dancing as if she weighed nothing at all. While she danced, Frida told her new friend all her secret problems.

Many years later, when Frida Kahlo was a famous artist, she remembered the imaginary little girl: "I do not

remember her image or her color. But I do know that
she laughed a lot. From my voice she knew everything
about me. How long had I been with her? I do not
know. It could have been a second or thousands of
years. . . . I was happy."

Frida cherished the memory of what she called her
"magic friendship." The imaginary child was her first
great creative act, and it foreshadowed her career as a
portrait artist. The self-portraits she painted, and for
which she is best known, are obviously of herself, but
they also reveal the little girl who was probably the best
friend she ever would have. Frida's paintings became
the "door" through which she slipped to find the safety
provided by her childhood daydream.

Children with imaginary playmates often have no sib-
lings and create a friend to make them feel less lonely.
Although Frida, the second youngest of six girls, was
hardly an only child, she often felt like an outcast and
hungered for someone who understood her. Only her
father made her feel as if she belonged, although he, too,
often felt different not only from his family but from the
Mexican people as well. Wilhelm Kahl, a Hungarian-Ger-
man Jew, was a student at the University of Nuremberg
when he suffered a serious fall, which at the time doctors
believed left him with severe epilepsy. More likely he fell
because he already possessed an undiagnosed case of the
disease. At nineteen, with dreams of scholarship destroyed
by the illness, he left Germany to start a new life in Mexico, an adventurous move for a young man of uncertain
health, little money, and no knowledge of Spanish. Wilhelm Kahl never returned home.

When he reached Mexico City, Wilhelm promptly
changed his first and last names to the Spanish-sounding

Guillermo Kahlo. He became an atheist and married a woman who died giving birth to their second child. The future looked bleak for this poor, ill man who had no profession but had two little daughters to support.

Although Mexico is composed of European and Indian cultures, the people are mostly homogeneous: they speak Spanish, practice Catholicism, and almost everyone is dark-skinned, dark-eyed, and dark-haired. As much as the blue-eyed Jewish Guillermo, with a German accent and stiff manner, wanted to be part of his adopted country, he felt that he never truly belonged.

On the night of his wife's death, he met Matilde Calderon, a pretty Spanish-Indian woman, and they soon married. For reasons that are not known, Matilde did not want Guillermo's young daughters, Maria Luisa and Margarita, to live with them. They were sent to a convent school and only occasionally visited their father and his four new daughters, Matilde, Adriana, Frida, and Cristina.

Guillermo's father-in-law, a photographer, encouraged Guillermo to join him in his business, and their first project was to travel throughout Mexico photographing its colonial architecture. Kahlo's meticulous, straightforward photographs, done in preparation for the 1910 centennial of Mexican independence, were beautiful, and he soon became well-known as the country's first official photographer.

Kahlo bought a plot of land in Coyoacan, a village an hour from his studio in Mexico City, and he built a house unlike anything he had ever seen in his boyhood in Germany. Two blocks from the large town plaza and park, the stucco house was a tall U-shaped one-story building. Each room opened onto a courtyard shaded with plants and trees.

Mexico City has an almost perfect climate. At seven

thousand feet it is warm during the day, cool at night, and rarely humid. Except during the summer, when it rains almost every day, it is comfortable to be outside most of the time. In such a place a garden becomes part of one's home, and people spend more of their lives in the natural world. The garden at the Kahlo house was such a part of Frida's consciousness that she often included its courtyard in the backgrounds of her paintings, especially the ones that were celebrations of life.

Frida was born on a rainy day, July 6, 1907, in the house her father had built three years before. As a child she spent much time climbing trees and playing in the garden. She returned to the house to live as a married woman, and she died in it. Like her immigrant father Frida struggled to know who she was and to find her place in the world, and with all its memories the house in Coyoacan gave her a sense of belonging. Still solid and handsome, the old house is now the Frida Kahlo Museum. How fitting that the house her father built, which sheltered her for most of her life, should someday shelter her paintings.

Every day Matilde took her daughters to church in the town square and insisted on prayers at meals. A stern though caring mother, Matilde had little difficulty disciplining her daughters—except for one. While the two older girls shut their eyes and concentrated on their prayers, Matilde always caught Frida teasing her little sister, Cristi, trying to make her laugh.

No matter how much Frida tried, she could not be like her obedient sisters, and though she wished that she and her mother could be closer, her mother's powerful will frightened her. She knew her mother wouldn't allow her father's daughters to live with them, and after she had seen her drown a litter of rats in the basement, she decided her mother was a cruel woman.

One of Matilde's harshest decisions was in response to her eldest daughter's elopement at fifteen. "Matita" was her favorite, and Matilde became hysterical when she discovered her daughter had run off. Frida had helped her sister escape by closing the window afterward, "as if nothing had happened." Matilde refused to let her daughter visit, but the younger Matilde tried for a while to keep her link to the family by leaving little baskets of fruit at the door. Eventually Matilde stopped coming to the house. Guillermo never protested his wife's decision, yet he missed his daughter. After a year he confided to Frida, "We'll never find her!" Twelve years later Senora Kahlo finally forgave her daughter and allowed Matilde to come home again.

Perhaps because she felt distant from her mother, Frida demonstrated her independent, sometimes rebellious, spirit early. During her first week of kindergarten, when the teacher turned off the lights and drew the shades to make the room dark for a demonstration, Frida looked at Cristina for reassurance, but her little sister's white face and saucer eyes didn't help. The teacher held up a candle in one hand and an orange in the other and explained how the sun, the earth, and the moon related to one another. Overwhelmed by the darkness and the amazing information, Frida wet her pants. When the teacher changed them using a dry pair that belonged to a girl who lived across the street from Frida, she instantly hated the girl. One day, as the girl passed by the Kahlo house, Frida jumped out and grabbed her by the throat. "Her tongue was already out of her mouth when a baker passed by and freed her from my hands," Frida recalled.

She demonstrated a demonic lack of constraint at home, also. Frida pushed one of her sisters off a chamber pot, and both went flying. Frida's mirth was cut short when her sister screamed, "You are not the daughter of my mother or my father. They picked you up out of a trash can!" Frida later said that this remark made her a "completely introverted creature." Soon afterward she "met" her imaginary friend.

More likely Frida turned inward because of the polio that struck her at six years old. It began with terrible pain in her right leg and forced her to be housebound for nine months. Polio, then the most dreaded disease of childhood, often crippled or killed children. Several times a day Frida's mother and older sisters washed her leg in a small tub with walnut water and hot towels, hoping to cure her of the disease.

For someone who was constantly moving, preferring to run, jump, and skip instead of walk, polio placed a new burden on Frida. Because she couldn't play with her sisters and friends, she became a brooder and a day-dreamer. She worried about whether or not she would walk again, about her mother, who didn't understand her, and about her father, who often brooded as well. She was grateful to the imaginary dancing girl who listened to her problems and kept her entertained.

When Frida went back to school, children stared at her thin right leg and slight limp, and the ruder ones teased her. No longer a sturdy, self-confident imp, Frida became shy, inhibited by her imperfection, which she tried to hide with extra socks and a special shoe with a higher heel. As soon as she was able to go outdoors, her father took her to Chapultepec Park in Mexico City, where he encouraged her to climb trees and row in the large lake that runs through the park. As she gradually began to walk again without a limp, she became even closer to her father; they shared the experience of illness, and she was grateful to him for helping her.

Of all the Kahlo girls, only Frida, baptized Magdalena Carmen Frida Kahlo y Calderon, bore a name reminiscent of her father's background. Frida spelled her name with an *e*, the German way, until 1932, when Hitler's rise to power made her want to sever any connection to Germany. *Frieda* means peace in German, and though Frida was anything but peaceful, she was her father's favorite. As a grown woman Frida would look back and say, "My childhood was marvelous, because although my father was a sick man (he had vertigos every month and a half), he was an immense example to me of tenderness, of work (photographer and also painter) and above all, of understanding for all my problems."

Guillermo adored his daughter and once said, "Frida is the most intelligent of my daughters, the most like me." But he was not a particularly accessible father to any of his children. At night, when he returned home from his studio, he played the piano in a room by himself, read philosophy, and ate his dinner alone. Only Frida, with her curiosity and high spirits, pulled him out of his solitude and stimulated him to teach her how to observe and consider things, especially in nature. Together they collected leaves, stones, shells, and insects, which Frida later examined under a microscope in her father's studio. These early lessons helped her to paint in precise and accurate detail. Herr Kahlo's tubes of oil paints and brushes that he dabbled with on weekends also captured Frida's attention. She longed to squeeze the bright colors onto the rough white canvases in the corner and slide the brush across the surface. But she knew better than to ask for permission that would certainly be denied.

Frida often accompanied her father on photographic assignments, because his seizures came without warning, leaving him helpless. As her father had helped her recover from polio, so she helped him to deal with his illness.

Guillermo Kahlo was grateful for his daughter's assistance, but his work decreased, not because of his ability but because of the Mexican Revolution in 1910. Mexico had begun its liberation in 1810 when it revolted against Spanish rule and, for the ensuing 100 years, the country had suffered dictatorships and instability under civilian as well as foreign command. From 1855 to 1872, Benito Juarez led Mexico toward a modern economy and social institutions, expanded rail, road, and telegraph networks, and developed secular education. His successor, Porfirio Diaz, continued the country's economic progress, but at the expense of liberty; furthermore, he allowed prosperity to reach only a small group of primarily foreign investors.

Pancho Villa and Emiliano Zapata led the revolt against Diaz' government in an attempt to improve the lives of the poor, but not everyone benefitted from the righteousness of their cause. Guillermo Kahlo depended upon commissions from the government under the corrupt president, Porfirio Diaz, to photograph different parts of the country. The revolution put an end to those commissions, and the family struggled to survive by taking boarders into the large house.

Despite their hardship the Kahlos sympathized with the tumultuous revolution, which would last ten years. As an adult Frida wrote in her diary, "I witnessed with my own eyes Zapata's peasants' battle against the Carrancistas. My mother opened the windows on Allende Street [the house was at the corner of Allende and Londres streets]. She gave access to the Zapatistas, seeing to it that the wounded and hungry jumped [through] the windows of my house into the living room. She cured them and gave them thick tortillas, the only food that could be obtained in Coyoacan in those days. In 1914 bullets just hissed. I still hear their extraordinary sound."

Mexico possessed rich natural resources, but the wealth always remained with only a few. Lighter-skinned European descendants lived in comfort, some in luxury, while the great majority of the people lived in grinding poverty. As a teenager Frida changed her birth date from 1907 to 1910, to declare her sympathies with the revolution and to link her birth with the beginnings of modern Mexico.

Most of Frida's two hundred paintings explore her identity and her vision of herself. The portrait *My Grandparents, My Parents, and I*, done in 1936, reveals the security that Frida's early family experiences gave her. The painting is a family tree, with her maternal grandparents in the upper left, her paternal grandparents in the upper right, her parents in the center, and Frida below them all. Frida is in front of her father, as though he is her protector.

Frida, a sturdy, round-faced, naked toddler holding a veinlike red ribbon that ties her to her ancestors, stands in the courtyard, encircled by her house. She shows her trademark single eyebrow that runs above one eye to the other, which she appears to inherit from her father's mother, the only ancestor with this trait. A little orange tree, heavy with fruit, grows beside her. The portrait depicts a time when Frida felt strong and in possession of herself as well as all that surrounded her.

The painting also reveals Frida's internal and external

dualities. In it she resembles her maternal grandfather, who is dark-skinned with high cheekbones and clearly belongs to the part of Mexico with which Frida most allied herself: the Aztec-Mayan Indian culture that preceded the Spanish conquest in the sixteenth century. The other grandfather is gray-haired, with a wide forehead and intense, intelligent blue eyes; he looks ready to jump off the canvas. Her father has the same searching eyes, and though Frida's eyes were brown, she always said she had her father's eyes and her mother's body.

Her parents are dressed in their wedding clothes, which makes the visible fetus in her mother's womb especially dramatic. The painting is all about Frida, who appears three times: as a baby, as an embryo, and at the moment of conception. Just below the ribbon on the left are an egg and sperm.

The house is blue, a color typical of a peasant house, and it was the color Frida painted the house in Coyoacan when she returned as an adult. When her parents lived there, the house was white and decorated with muted colors, draperies, and dark, heavy furniture, European styles typical of Mexican middle- and upper-class homes.

Like Frida the painting is rich with paradox. In the background on the left are the vegetation and mountains of Mexico: this was her land, and these were the people who gave her strength. But on the right is the ocean that her father had crossed from Europe. Of all her self-portraits this one shows Frida at her most secure and contented, with no hint of nightmares. As she grew up, the security of the red ribbon, tying her to home and family, would not be enough to protect her from her pain and sorrow.

CHAPTER 2

LAS CACHUCHAS

AT FOURTEEN Frida still sat dutifully at her mother's prayer meetings and allowed herself to be taken to church, but her mind was usually far away; she was aching to taste life outside her family. Just as the revolution had progressed beyond the rifle and had begun to change people's lives, Frida had also moved from rebellion to a deeper focus by the time she entered high school. She loved her family and believed in the Church, but she wanted a broader world than the one in which she had been raised. Frida's father, her ally in helping her on this path, hoped Frida would fulfill his dreams of scholarship.

The National Preparatory School in Mexico City was the best school in Latin America. Part of the National University, it enjoyed a reputation for rigorous curriculum and for educating Mexico's future leadership; though it was only a high school, it demanded the equivalent of a university today. Matilde Kahlo had not

sent any of her daughters to this school and didn't know
why Frida, who would surely marry and have children,
just as almost every Mexican woman did, needed such
schooling. A good mother, Matilde had already taught
her daughters how to cook, sew, and clean, and she
believed that those skills plus their Catholic education
was all they needed to know. Besides, the bus ride to
school was an hour each way from Coyoacan, and she
didn't want Frida so far from home. But Guillermo
Kahlo had great hopes for his *lieber Frieda* (dear, loving
Frida). Despite the long ride, and despite that among the
two thousand students who attended the school only
thirty-five were girls, he was determined for Frida to get
the best education Mexico had to offer.

Frida needed no prodding to go to the National Preparatory School. In addition to offering her a superior education, the school would put her in Mexico City, the
heart of the Mexican Revolution. On the first day of
school, Frida entered the tall red-brick building through
massive doors that foretold seriousness and purpose.
Inside the entrance a graceful courtyard greeted her, and
as she looked up, enormous, dramatic murals painted
on the walls of the building caught her eye. Her father
had taught her well by encouraging her to look deeply,
and now she was in a place where there would be much
to see and absorb.

With a curriculum leading to medical school, an
unusually ambitious and expensive goal for anyone of
the middle class, but especially for a woman, Frida
strode into school, head held high, dressed like a female
counterpart of her father in his university days in Nuremberg. In a school where there were no uniforms, Frida
wore a white blouse, a dark blue pleated gabardine skirt,

thick stockings, boots, and a black straw hat, the typical uniform of a German schoolgirl. Her thick black eyebrows, long eyelashes, and intense eyes completed the picture of a determined young woman.

In a heavy knapsack Frida carried a notebook with drawings, pinned butterflies and dried flowers, colored pens, and philosophy books from her father's library. In the spirit of the Revolution, Frida was beginning to embrace the Indian blood that she inherited from her mother, but when it came to intellect, her father remained her guide.

In Mexico City, Frida saw how the Revolution was taking place in nonmilitary ways. Half-Indian Porfirio Diaz despised native Mexican culture and, like many in Mexico, followed the trend of lightening his face with powder to look more European. Alvaro Obregon, the new president, had ousted those government officials who worshiped Europe as the intellectual and cultural model for Mexico. The new minister of education, Jose Vasconcelos, proclaimed Mexican education to be about "our blood, our language, and our people."

The Revolution helped form Frida's personality as she identified with it intellectually, emotionally, and spiritually. Andreas Iduarte, one of Frida's classmates who later became the director of the National Institute of Fine Arts, wrote of the Preparatoria days: "We were fortunate, together with Frida, we were fortunate, the young people, the boys, the children of my time: our vitality coincided with that of Mexico; we grew spiritually while the country grew in the moral realm."

Despite her European father, whom she adored, Frida's style became consciously revolutionary. After a few months Frida stopped dressing like a German schoolgirl and began to wear overalls. She cut her thick black hair into bangs, like a boy, and sped around Coyoacan on a bicycle. Frida's mother must have cringed when other mothers remarked, *"Que nina tan fea!"* (What an ugly little girl!) but neither Matilde, nor anyone else, could influence Frida's radical new look.

At school, however, Frida fit in perfectly. She thrived on the intellectual and cultural stimulation at the National Prep, and for the first time she didn't feel like a misfit. She developed *cuates*, pals who were her soul mates, some of whom would remain lifelong friends. Most were boys, because Frida didn't want to be part of the gossipy and frivolous girls' group, and her *cuates* admired her free spirit instead of condemning it.

Like a magnet Frida attracted anyone who possessed both brains and spirit. She quickly became part of the notorious Cachuchas, a group of seven boys and two girls named for the rowboat-shaped hats they wore; the club was notorious for its members' intelligence and capacity for trouble. Despite her intelligence Frida didn't care much about her studies or pleasing teachers, and she openly cut class if she found it boring. Her mischievous nature as a child made it easy for her to be daring. Even the boys admired her courage, and Frida soon became the chief Cachucha. The group shared a mistrust of authority, and an indifference to anything their elders revered. Their pranks expressed their disdain for the establishment, particularly at school, because they believed all institutions represented the old, corrupt way.

One day the Cachuchas let a donkey loose in a classroom. Another time classes were disrupted when a dog ran through the school barking wildly to get away from fireworks that someone had set off next to him. Everyone knew who the culprits were. The worst victim of the Cachuchas was Antonio Caso, a renowned professor. His only "sin" was an exclusive adoration of ancient philosophers such as Aristotle and Socrates, and an ignorance of Lenin and Marx, instigators of the Russian Revolution. Frida wanted Caso fired. Unable to accomplish that, she helped her cohorts light a firecracker outside his room while he lectured on evolution. Jose Gomez Robleda, a Cachucha who later became a professor of psychiatry, lit the fuse. He remembered, "I stayed [and lit the fuse] and sat down in the Generalito next to the prefect of the girl students. After a while came the explosion. *Baroom!* The glass windowpanes broke, and a hail of glass and stones and gravel fell on Antonio Caso." The professor didn't miss a beat, though. He just dusted himself off and continued with his lecture. Later Caso would fall prey, unwittingly, to another of Frida's escapades.

When bored, Frida amused herself by drawing pictures of her teachers in class and passing them around the room. Her best was a dozing elephant, resembling a psychology professor, giving a drowsy lecture about sleep. After one too many escapades, Frida was expelled from school, but her fearlessness saved her. She went directly to the minister of education, Vasconcelos, and told him that she had been unfairly banished by the principal of the school. The minister was no friend of the principal and took advantage of the situation to thwart him. "If you can't manage a little girl like that," he warned the principal, "then you are not fit to be a director of such an institution."

Frida remained in school, but much of her education took place outside the classroom, in the Zocalo, a huge plaza just a couple of blocks from the school. The square, surrounded by a cathedral and graceful buildings, teemed with street life. Homeless newsboys bearing heavy loads on their backs taught her how to swear; little girls selling dolls they had embroidered and young boys pushing carts of food and shouting, *"Churros! Mil pesos! Empanadas aqui!"* all became her friends.

The Cachuchas were Frida's other education. At the Ibero-American Library, housed in a church near the school, the group hung out to talk, plan their escapades, and read. In the pre-TV 1920s, books provided not only information but also a primary source of entertainment and recreation. Frida and her friends raced one another to finish their books first, and sometimes they played games with them. When they read fantasies by authors such as Jules Verne or H. G. Wells, or stories of far-off places, each Cachucha invented an imaginary journey to tell the others, offering minute detail of what it was like, for example, to travel along the bottom of the ocean or climb the Himalayas in India. Books liberated Frida from the narrow world of Coyoacan. By the time she was sixteen, she read not only in Spanish, but in German and English, and learned through books about the lives of artists and of revolutions in other times and places.

If lectures didn't compel Frida, the exterior walls of the school, which had attracted her from the first day of school, also became her teacher. In 1921 and 1922 the Revolution, in the form of art, reached the Preparatoria. Vasconcelos commissioned artists to decorate the walls of the school with frescoes, paintings drawn on freshly plastered walls. With Mexican history as their subject, artists worked to transform society.

Traditionally, art had been a privilege of the wealthy and educated. They could own it or, in their leisure, go see it in museums. A street vendor, however, or a mother with nine children had no time or money to visit museums and enjoy the pleasure and enlightenment of art. Murals on public walls enriched everyone's life, young and old, rich and poor. The murals going up all over Mexico provided more than beautiful adornments; they educated poor workers and peasants about Mexican history and showed the dignity and righteousness of Mexican culture, fostering pride in the people. It was hoped that art could inspire social change. Since the opportunity to influence a person is strongest in the young, schools were an especially important place for murals. Classes in art and history became more relevant as the paintings reflected the lessons of the classroom.

In 1922 the most famous painter in Mexico and certainly among the most renowned in the world, Diego Rivera, began a mural in the Preparatoria's auditorium. Rivera had lived in Europe for fifteen years, and this was his first important public work at home in Mexico. Women adored him and followed him everywhere, despite the fact that he was thirty-six, had bulging eyes, puffy lips, and weighed three hundred pounds.

Frida was fascinated by Rivera. Students weren't allowed into the auditorium while "El Maestro" worked, but that didn't stop Frida, who hid as she watched him for hours. Once, while he painted on the stage, Frida sneaked in and soaped the steps he would have to descend after work. Concealed behind a pillar, she waited to see the fat man slip and slide. But Rivera, moving slowly the way large people often do, did not lose his footing. The next day the unfortunate professor, Antonio Caso, who had endured a firecracker in his class, took the fall intended for Diego.

As Frida watched Rivera work, she teased him about the women in his life. When Lupe Marin, his wife, visited him in the auditorium, Frida, hiding in the back, would shout, "Look out, Panzon (fat belly)—Nahui's coming!" Of course, Nahui, his current girlfriend, was nowhere in sight. Neither Rivera nor Lupe Marin had any idea who this impudent and nosy student was.

Frida had a crush on Diego and wanted his attention, but no one could understand it. One day she told her best friend, Adelina Zendejas, "My only ambition is to have a child by Diego Rivera, the painter. And I'm going to tell him so some day."

Adelina looked at her with shock. "But Frida, he's so disgusting! He's potbellied, filthy, terrible looking. I'm afraid of him."

Frida shook her head and answered, "Diego is so gentle, so tender, so wise, so sweet. I'd bathe him and clean him." Frida would one day get the chance to give Diego a bath, but until then all she could do was sit for hours and watch him work. He ignored her, perhaps because her small, compact figure made her look younger than her fourteen years.

Frida was not going to be lonely while waiting for "Panzon" to notice her. Her great love was not the unattainable Diego but Alejandro Gomez Arias, a member of the Cachuchas. A few years older than Frida, Alejandro was handsome, popular, athletic, and intellectual; he soon became her first *novio* (boyfriend). In his old age Alejandro would remember Frida as having "a fresh, perhaps ingenuous, childlike manner, but at the same time she was quick and dramatic in her urge to discover life."

Because Frida was afraid of what her mother might do if she found out about her romance, she kept it a secret by seeing Alejandro alone only briefly. Frida put her inventive mind to work and wrote Alejandro witty, passionate letters that revealed her feelings not only for him but for everything in life. Boldly candid, the letters were adorned with drawings, fancy script, and bits of English language. In one letter she drew a girl with a long neck, pointed chin, and huge eyes, in the elongated style of Modigliani, and wrote beside it: "Don't tear her, because she is very pretty. [This is] an ideal type." Lower on the page she drew a cat and wrote: "Another ideal type."

As their relationship warmed, the letters grew more passionate. "Tell me if you don't love me anymore Alex, I love you even if you do not love me as much as a flea," she wrote. She signed her letters with a triangle or full lipstick kisses. When Frida was sick and couldn't see Alejandro, she begged Cristina to mail her daily letters at the post office, and in order to fool her family, she had Alejandro sign his letters "Agustina Reyna." As much as Frida's letters to Alejandro revealed her feeling for him, they also disclosed her intense and passionate nature. The letters she wrote to anyone she cared about made the recipient feel Frida would die without his or her love. She loved being in love, and she lifted her partner to an equal level of feeling. Her letters carried magic, and combined with her physical beauty, they made her hard to resist. If Alejandro had not been so sure of himself and equally strong as Frida, he could have become her toy. In fact, he became one of Mexico's great independent intellectuals, the first of a series of remarkable people who were part of Frida's life.

Whenever the Revolution flared up and there was fighting in the city, Frida's mother insisted she stay home in Coyoacan. She hated missing the action and wrote Alejandro: "Tell me what's new in Mexico [City], about your life and about everything that you want to tell me since you know that here there is nothing but pasture and pasture, Indians and Indians, and huts and huts. . . ."

Other letters from Frida to Alejandro resemble a diary, with long descriptions of arguments in the family, especially between her and Cristina. She also dreamed of going to America with Alejandro: "Listen little brother now in 1925 we are going to love each other a lot eh? Forgive the repetition of the word 'love.' 5 times in one go but I am very gushy. Don't you think that we should keep on carefully planning the trip to the United States, I want you to tell me how you feel about going in December of this year, there is lots of time to arrange things do you agree? Tell me all the pros and cons and whether you really can go, because look Alex; it is good that we should do something in life don't you think so, since we'll be nothing but dopes if we spend our whole life in Mexico, because for me there is nothing more lovely than to travel."

Unfortunately, Frida's chances of travel were slim because her family's finances were so uncertain. She had to take a job as a cashier in a pharmacy in her last year of school. Because she could never get the cash register to agree with the amount of money in its drawer, she tried other jobs, mostly secretarial, at which she was not very successful, either.

Her father found her a job with his friend, Fernando Fernandez, a printer. Frida's talent for drawing, which amused her friends in school and enchanted Alejandro in her letters, emerged with Fernandez, who saw that Frida possessed unusual talent in copying prints for engraving. Although Frida was still anxious to see the world, her work with Fernandez satisfied her, and she dreamed of saving some of her earnings for her trip with Alejandro. After what happened to her older sister when she ran away with her boyfriend, Frida was careful not to let her mother know her plans. By the time Frida was eighteen, she was no longer a child, and she felt she had outgrown middle-class Catholicism and suburbia. Although she still prayed, she had long ago given up confessions, and she was moving away from her family and toward friends closer to her own ideals and feelings.

In 1925 Guillermo Kahlo took a family portrait, quite formal, with everyone dressed up. The older women dressed in dark dresses, the girls in light dresses. Frida's mother sits in the middle of the picture, solid and proud, but hardly looking like the mother of the young woman on the left. Frida is the most dominant figure in the picture, wearing a man's suit, her hair pulled back. She looks powerfully into the camera, challenging the viewer to accept her.

Frida makes the photograph intriguing and unique. By raising questions through her cross dressing, her open sensuality, and her confrontational attitude, the picture becomes more than a conventional portrait—it

becomes a political statement. Frida seems to commu-
nicate that she wants the freedom and independence
of a man, and that she also wants to unsettle, even
shock, the viewer. ''Pay attention to me, I'm different,'' she seems to be saying. ''I want you to know
me.'' The surprise and intimacy she creates in the portrait would later mark Frida's work.

CHAPTER 3

Accident

IN 1925, her senior year at the Preparatoria, Frida began to make plans to go to medical school, hoping that her father would somehow find the money for tuition. Eager to explore the world and ready for the challenge of adulthood, she appeared to be full of confidence to those who knew her. Not only pretty and bright, she had the most coveted boyfriend at school. Still, not everyone liked her, and among the more conservative students, especially girls, Frida was considered "fast." Although she had lost her reputation as a devout and virtuous girl, Frida didn't care about the opinions of others. As she wrote Alejandro, "It's not important to me. I like who I am."

A rainy day in September robbed Frida of the future she had dreamed of and planned. The day also taught her how strong she was. Frida never minded the long distance she traveled by train to and from school every day. In her senior year a bus began operating between

Coyoacan and Mexico City; eager to enjoy the speed and comfort of this latest technology, Frida switched her transportation to the bus. The drivers were macho and sometimes careless, but teenaged Frida, believing she was invincible, never worried about safety.

Frida loved it when a friend joined her on the ride, and on that September day Alejandro rode with her on the freshly painted wooden bus back to Coyoacan in the late afternoon. They pushed their way to two seats in the back and started their usual intense conversations about school and politics, or about German philosophers such as Spengler and Schopenhauer. As the lurching bus crossed in front of the San Juan market a few blocks from school, a trolley turned onto the street where the bus was crossing, and though both vehicles were going very slowly, neither yielded to the other. As it rounded the corner, the trolley pushed the bus against the wall, stretching and crushing it.

Many years later Frida would say: "I was an intelligent young girl, but impractical, in spite of all the freedom I had won. Perhaps for this reason I did not assess the situation, nor did I guess the kind of wounds I had. The first thing I thought of was the *balero* [Mexican toy] with pretty colors that I had bought that day and that I was carrying with me. I tried to look for it, thinking that what had happened would not have major consequences.

"It is a lie that one is aware of the crash, a lie that one cries. In me there were no tears. The crash bounced us forward, and a handrail pierced me the way a sword pierces a bull. A man saw me having a tremendous hemorrhage. He carried me and put me on a billiard table until the Red Cross came for me."

Alejandro and Frida would remember the catastrophe

all their lives. And Frida, who would later often paint violent visual images, never had the courage to paint the accident that mutilated her body. The seats of the bus were long benches on either side, and when the metal trolley crashed into the wooden bus, the bus stretched so much, Alejandro's knees touched the person sitting opposite him. "I was sitting next to Frida," he said. "When the bus reached its maximal flexibility, it burst into a thousand pieces, and the train kept moving. It ran over many people."

When the bus exploded, bodies flew in all directions. Alejandro was thrown under the trolley. Although he was badly cut and bleeding, he was able to get up and look for Frida, but he could hardly bear what he saw. Frida was impaled on a steel rod running entirely through her body. Her clothes had blown off from the impact of the explosion, and she was naked, with only blood covering her. Even more horrible, Frida looked otherworldly because someone on the bus, most likely an artist or a painter, had been carrying gold dust, and the gold was glistening on Frida's body, already shiny with blood. Mexican culture accepts, even embraces, the magical or surreal. Life and death are closely linked in agricultural societies; fresh green shoots are part of the dying tree from which they emerge, so death, therefore, is not ugly. When people rushed up to the scene of the accident and saw Frida bathed in red and gold, they screamed, *"La bailarina, la bailarina!"* In the midst of gory catastrophe, they saw not a dying woman covered with blood and gold dust, but a beautiful dancer.

A workman from the school came by, took one look at Frida, and grabbed Alejandro, saying, "We have to take that metal out of her." He put a knee on Frida's body and pulled on the steel rod. Unfortunately Frida remained conscious and she screamed more loudly than the siren of the approaching Red Cross ambulance. Alejandro, certain she was going to die, helped to lift her onto the table and put his coat over her naked body.

In the Red Cross hospital, doctors and nurses quickly examined the scores of victims, sending them into two rooms, separating the injured—who received immediate help—from the dying. Frida, bleeding profusely and with a gaping hole through her abdomen, was in the latter group. "Frida's condition was so grave that the doctors did not think they could save her," Alejandro recalled. "They thought she would die on the operating table."

When Frida's mother and father heard about their daughter's accident, they were devastated. Matilde could not speak for a month after the accident, and Frida's father became ill. At first neither parent visited Frida in the hospital, and they were so poor they couldn't imagine how they would pay the medical bills. Perhaps Frida's paintings, created a decade after the accident, filled with blood and pain, were an unconscious way of showing her parents what they had missed. Eventually her mother and father were able to visit her a few times, but Frida could hardly bear their suffering. "To have given them this blow hurt me more than forty wounds," Frida told Alejandro. "My mother was like a crazy woman with tears for three days."

Frida's survival was a miracle. She suffered a spine broken in three places, a broken collarbone, and two broken ribs. Her right leg was shattered, broken in eleven places, and her right foot had been crushed. Her left shoulder was dislocated, and her pelvis was broken in three places. She would never have a day without pain for the rest of her life. Frida survived, but more than her body needed to heal. The shock of confronting her fragility, life's potential for suffering, and the recognition that she would never be the same, had weakened her spirit.

Frida's older sister, Matilde, read about the accident in the newspaper and immediately rushed to the hospital, delighted to see her little sister again after so many years, but horrified by the circumstances. Frida was in a plaster cast within a large coffinlike box, unable to move anything but her head. In a ward with twenty-five other patients and only one nurse, if Frida needed her nose scratched or a drink of water, she had to wait a long time. Slowly, during the endless days of recuperation, Frida began to understand that her life had been irrevocably changed. Alone with her pain most of the time, she was gradually learning that despite her broken body, her powerful and curious spirit had stayed alive. She joked with the nurses and asked questions about her condition.

Matilde came every day to be with her younger sister. Frida said, "It was Matilde who lifted my spirits; she told me jokes. She was fat and ugly, but she had a great sense of humor. She made everyone in the room howl with laughter." The Cachuchas also visited and cheered her up, but when she was alone, fear became her visitor. She wrote Alejandro, "In this hospital death dances every night around my bed."

After a month Frida left the hospital, knowing she had months of bed rest ahead. Much as she was glad to leave, she dreaded going home. With school nearby, the hospital had been an easy place for her friends to visit her, but it was much too far for them to go to her home. Because Matilde was still banished from the family, she couldn't be with her anymore, either. Her father's depression and her mother's constant bad moods caused Frida to describe her family as "one of the saddest that I have seen."

During Frida's three months in bed, she began to try to make sense of her accident, an endeavor that would last the rest of her life. How would she, a person friends described as seeming "to float like a bird in flight," endure the burden of chronic pain? How would the accident permanently disfigure her? Would friends turn away from a changed Frida? She no longer could conjure up her dancing friend to console her.

Frida had stumbled upon a terrifying truth that none of her contemporaries understood yet: a split second can change one's life, and there is no way to negotiate or compromise the moment. She wrote Alejandro, "Now I live in a painful planet, transparent as ice; but it is as if I had learned everything at once in seconds. My friends, companions, became women slowly, I became old in an instant, and everything today is bland and lucid. I know that nothing lies ahead; if there were something, I would see it." Born of frustration with her situation, despair became another battle that dogged Frida. Later, friends would describe the joyfulness of her spirit, her deep, frequent laughter and jokes, yet at the same time they acknowledged that her paintings revealed a darker part of her.

Frida's close encounter with death had terrified her. Every time she felt a pain or became ill, she was seized with panic that she would die. She began to call death *la pelona,* which means "the bald or stupid woman," in order to triumph over her fear. "I tease and laugh at death," she told a friend, "so it won't get the better of me." Frida was fortunate in that she lived in a society that doesn't shy away from death but allows it to be part of life. There are streets in Mexico with names such as Ravine of the Dead, and in November all of Latin America celebrates Dia de los Muertos (Day of the Dead) with people dressed up as skeletons, skulls, and dark hooded figures, all representing death. This is not a somber holiday, but one filled with good food, drink, and special treats for children, such as sugar skulls and skeleton cookies.

Frida, who had always loved Dia de los Muertos, now embraced its customs for new purposes. She didn't want death, or her fear of it, to take away her laughter or joy in life, so she dressed cardboard skeletons in her clothes, called death by insulting nicknames, and had a skull painted with her name on it, all in an effort to defy suffering and death. Giant Judas (pronounced *hoo-dahs*) figures also took on fresh meaning for Frida. The huge papier-mâché puppets, lined with fireworks, usually in the form of a devil or skeleton to represent sin and death, are part of the celebration of Saturday of Glory, which falls on the Saturday before Easter. As despised enemies the figures are exploded in the town square to boisterous cheers, and in the year following her accident, Frida cheered loudest of all—she had defied death once and was determined to extend her victory into a very long life.

The accident surely changed Frida physically, but the struggle to find a new direction for her life is what changed her personality. The most dramatic difference was that it made her extraordinarily aware of her body—when it worked well, when it hurt, how others saw her. Frida, who had always been vain, became even more self-absorbed in her condition and treatment. Despite her

exasperation at being immobile, it taught her how to be
still and to observe what went on around her. It gave
her time to face her life that was filled not only with
sadness and pain, but also with courage and honesty.
She told Alejandro, "One must put up with it. I am
beginning to grow accustomed to suffering." She hadn't
lost her sense of humor and her capacity for delight, but
she had learned that everything, including grief and joy,
is temporary. She wrote Alejandro constantly, perhaps
because she had few visitors and so little to do in a time
before television and the phone. Sometimes her letters
would be full of complaints: "I'm sick of these four
walls!" "I was born to be a flower pot and I never leave
the dining room!" Most of the time she wrote as she
had always written him, with passion, wit, and high
spirits: "Believe me, Alex, I want you to come, for I am
ready to go to the devil and I have no recourse but to
stand it since it is worse to get desperate don't you
think? I want you to come and chat with me like before,
for you to forget everything and for the love of your
saintly mother come and see me and tell me that you
love me even if it isn't true eh? (the pen doesn't write
well in tears.)" Frida wanted Alejandro to "forget everything" about Fernando Fernandez, the man to whom
she was apprenticed; Alejandro had found out she had
gone out with Fernandez, and he was hurt and jealous.

Three months after the accident, Frida was well
enough to travel to Mexico City. A photograph taken of
her by her father at this time shows a remarkably
healthy Frida, sitting up straight, characteristically looking directly, unsmiling, at the viewer. The only sign of
the accident is so subtle, it is almost unnoticeable. Frida
has crossed her strong left leg in front of the right, the

one made thin by polio and then later broken, so that the leg is barely in the picture. Her posture and face command full attention, however, and divert the viewer from her legs. She didn't want anyone to see her deformity or to know her pain. As her friend Adelina said, "If she cried, no one knew it."

In her lap Frida holds two books, perhaps evidence of her intention to pick up her life where it was interrupted by the accident. Yet she didn't sign up for more classes at school, because she needed to work to help her family pay her medical bills. The change of plans did not feel like a tragedy to Frida, however. "I felt I had energies to do anything instead of studying to become a doctor." Even a relapse a year after the accident did not discourage Frida, but she was put in another plaster cast, with orders not to move until her spine healed.

Alejandro saved Frida's letters, but because she didn't save his, there is no way of knowing how he felt about her at this time. Frida's letters suggest that she was losing her hold on him: "I am afraid that just as you did not tell me when you were leaving, you are deceiving me when you tell me that you are only going to be away for four months." Alejandro had left for Europe, apparently without telling Frida, perhaps because his family did not approve of her or because he may have been intimidated by her invalid condition.

Without Alejandro, school, or friends to absorb her, and with her exasperation at having to keep her body still while it healed, Frida turned to her father's hobby, painting. From the time she was a child, she struggled to resist the temptation to play with a box of oil paints and the brushes her father kept in an old vase in his photography studio. Like everything surrounding Guillermo Kahlo, the paints were neatly lined up in the box, and the brushes stood up next to one another perfectly straight. When Kahlo had the time, he enjoyed painting landscapes, especially the small river that runs through Coyoacan. Frida didn't know why painting appealed to her, but anything to do with her father was a powerful influence, and illness gave her the excuse to be bold. One day, when Guillermo visited her in bed, she asked if she could use his paints.

If anyone could get something from this introverted, fastidious man, it was Frida, though her father was still reluctant. As Frida described it, "Like a little boy whose toy is taken away from him and given to a sick brother, he 'lent' it to me." Maybe he thought Frida would be careless with the paints, since she was so confined by the body cast and had to remain prone, but her mother had a carpenter build a special easel so Frida could paint from her bed.

Besides the wickedly amusing pictures of teachers Frida had drawn in school, she occasionally made detailed drawings of slides she had seen under the microscope. She actually enjoyed this kind of drawing so much that she briefly considered a career in scientific illustration. Now, the first day she spread out the paints and faced an empty canvas, Frida wondered what to paint. Deciding that she could draw only what was near to her, she began by painting her friends and herself.

Frida became her own teacher, studying her father's art books and copying masters to learn technique. Her eye was good in spotting falseness, mediocrity, and greatness, and her instinct guided her. Botticelli and Modigliani, with their idealized women, can be found in her first attempts. Frida never became part of an artistic school or even a student of a famous painter, yet her work was sophisticated because of her wide knowledge of art. Perhaps because she was an autodidact, her work's uniqueness is one of its strongest qualities.

Frida's early portraits were gifts to friends, carefully painted and full of life, betraying no hint of sorrow. The subjects' posture is stiff and formal in the style of eighteenth-century portraits, with women wearing low-cut beautiful dresses. Her first self-portrait, done with the help of a mirror on the underside of the canopy of her bed, depicted more than Frida learning to paint. It was an entreaty to Alejandro. If her words couldn't hold him, perhaps he would fall in love with her again after he had a painting that captured her at her most lovable—and unbroken.

In the painting Frida looks directly at the viewer, in much the same way she posed for photographs. But this is not a fierce Frida; instead she is a gentle European-looking Frida, perhaps because she thought Alejandro's travels had changed his taste in women. The only unconventional, arresting part of the painting is her eyebrows, which are joined. Her neck is long, and the painting resembles Modigliani's style. Frida is wearing a red dress with a plunging neckline, but the picture is not really seductive. Her hand in the foreground seems to be held out for Alejandro, imploring him to return to her.

The accident never happened to the woman in this picture. Maybe she suspected that Alejandro wouldn't love her if she was less than perfect, so she painted flawlessness. Nothing in her eyes, face, or carriage betrays the pain, fear, or wisdom of her later works, and only the almost black background with ghostly clouds and towering waves suggests her inner world. The back of

the picture reads, "Frieda Kahlo at 17 years of age in
September 1926." Frida's real age at this time was
nineteen.

The painting also records: *Heute ist Immer Noch* (Today
still goes on). Life was going to be difficult because Frida
was always inclined to be rebellious, and her body
would require much of her attention. On the other hand,
her infirmity fascinated as well as frustrated her. At nineteen she knew that she wanted to live, to be part of life.
She could feel sorry for herself, but that wouldn't gain
her friends. If she wanted to be part of other people's
lives, she would have to appear in life like the self-portrait—a whole person. Because she despised pity, she
was determined not to let anyone see the scars under her
clothes and inside her heart. Using German, her father's
language, to express her decision to live suggests that
Guillermo Kahlo's determination to work, despite his illness, was an inspiration to her.

CHAPTER 4

Choosing Life

By the time Frida had recovered from the accident in 1927, her friends had already graduated from the Preparatoria and were in the university. Even though she didn't go to classes with them, she again joined her old group, the Cachuchas, participating in their political rallies and activities that were now more than teenage pranks. Their first major effort was to support minister of education Jose Vasconcelos's campaign for the presidency. Although he and his followers knew they didn't stand a chance against the military regime opposing him, Vasconcelos wanted to create a political party out of the Revolution for a democratic, modern society that had begun in the early twenties. Frida passionately fought for her old ally, but, as expected, he lost the election.

By this time Alejandro was no longer Frida's lover, but a friend. As a law student he had become a leader in the students' fight for a university independent of the government. The battle was serious, and the government brought in mounted police and weapons. Frida may not have been a student, but she believed in the cause and fought beside her comrades.

Frida became part of a circle of student revolutionaries, artists, and intellectuals, and she discovered a new adult world to which she yearned to belong. Her new political friends, who were primarily Communists, revolutionized her and provided her with another way of life. She didn't want to live like her mother, aunts, and sisters as a suburban housewife, yet without the goal of becoming a doctor, she couldn't count on her father to support her straying from a traditional woman's role.

Frida loved painting but was afraid to take it seriously. Was she any good? Who would buy her work? The only money Frida earned from art was as a teacher of young boys. She, who had no formal art lessons, had her students lie on the floor on their stomachs to draw, and joining them, Frida commanded, "Don't copy anyone! Paint your houses, your mothers, your brothers, the bus, *things that happen.*"

Tina Modotti, an American photographer who admired the people and politics of Mexico, befriended Frida. Modotti, beautiful, talented, and passionately political, was the first woman that Frida, at nineteen, wanted to model herself after. She cared about *la gente* (the people), hated how those in power exploited them, and used her art to expose injustice. Just as Frida would later wear the clothes of the Indian Tehuanas as a gesture of solidarity and identification, Modotti honored the peasants by photographing them.

Slowly Frida moved away from Alejandro's world of student politics and into a society of artists who were trying to create a new art and a new society. The Revolution of 1910 had given Mexico hope, and by the late twenties many students, teachers, and artists became political activists in their shared belief that it was possible to make *la raza* strong again by connecting them to their roots through education and art.

As Mexico began to appreciate its native culture, pride in its own history replaced European influence. Pre-Columbian art, which predated Columbus's discovery of the New World, once considered crude and primitive, was now found to be powerfully beautiful in its frank expression of life. Fertility goddesses with large breasts, small figures representing events in everyday life such as childbirth or a haircut, were part of that culture's art. Tequila and pulque (the poor man's tequila) replaced French wine, while mariachi music, folk art, and peasant clothing became the new style. Avant-garde mothers took to carrying their babies in *rebozos* (large shawls) instead of pushing them in English prams. Mexican artists, even those who had studied in Europe, proclaimed in a collaborative statement that Mexican art was "great because it surges from the people." The love of strong color, the acceptance of magic in everyday life, and the intimate connection with the land, were qualities all uniquely Mexican.

As part of the new society they were trying to create, artists wanted their work to be public property. In a manifesto declaring their sympathy with the people, they wrote, "The makers of beauty must invest their greatest efforts in the aim of materializing an art valuable to the people, and our supreme objective in art, which is today an expression for individual pleasure, is to create beauty for all, beauty that enlightens and stirs to struggle." Whether art helped to further the Revolution or simply reflected it is difficult to say, but certainly the creative efforts of the times stand as testament to a poor people gaining strength and dignity from the richness of *Mexicanidad*—what it is to be Mexican.

Jose Clemente Orozco, David Siquieros, and Diego Rivera, friends of Tina Modotti, were the artists responsible for mural renaissance and Mexico's prominent position in modern art in the thirties. Like most Mexican artists and intellectuals, they supported the Revolution and embraced Russian Communism as a model. Within a few months Frida joined the Communist party to express her ideals and to be part of the art world. More than political allies, the group served as family to its members, and they enjoyed frequent parties that helped them to break free from middle-class inhibition.

Although Frida was usually awed by the partygoers, one evening at Tina's she spotted the object of her schoolgirl crush, Diego Rivera. She couldn't take her eyes off him, especially when, at one point during the evening, Rivera whipped out his pistol and shot Tina's phonograph in the crowded room. Frida later said, "I began to be very interested in him in spite of the fear I had of him." Although she didn't speak to him that night, soon afterward Frida decided to visit "El Maestro," the man she had teased years ago. This time, however, she wanted more than his attention.

In his biography Rivera remembered their meeting this way: "Just before I went to Cuernavaca, there occurred one of the happiest events in my life. I was at work on one of the uppermost frescoes of the Ministry of Education, building one, when I heard a girl shouting up to me, 'Diego, please come down from there! I have something important to discuss with you!'

"I turned my head and looked down from my scaffold. On the ground beneath me stood a girl of about eighteen. She had a fine nervous body, topped by a delicate face. Her hair was long: dark and thick eyebrows met above her nose. They seemed like the wings of a blackbird, their black arches framing two extraordinary brown eyes.

"When I climbed down, she said, 'I didn't come here for fun. I have to work to earn my livelihood. I have done some paintings which I want you to look over professionally. I want an absolutely straightforward opinion, because I cannot afford to go on just to appease my vanity. I want you to tell me whether you think I can become a good enough artist to make it worth my while to go on. I've brought three of my paintings here. Will you come and look at them?'

" 'Yes,' I said, and followed her to a cubicle under a stairway where she had left her paintings. She turned each of them, leaning against the wall, to face me. They were all three portraits of women. As I looked at them, one by one, I was immediately impressed. The canvases revealed an unusual energy of expression, precise delineation of character, and true severity. They showed none of the tricks in the name of originality that usually mark the work of ambitious beginners. They had a fundamental plastic honesty, and an artistic personality of their own. They communicated a vital sensuality, complemented by a merciless yet sensitive power of observation. It was obvious to me that this girl was an authentic artist.

"She undoubtedly noticed the enthusiasm in my face, for before I could say anything, she admonished me in a harshly defensive tone. 'I have not come to you looking for compliments. I want the criticism of a serious man. I'm neither an art lover nor an amateur. I'm simply a girl who must work for her living.'

"I felt deeply moved by admiration for this girl. I had to restrain myself from praising her as much as I wanted to. Yet I could not be completely insincere. I was puzzled by her attitude. Why, I asked her, didn't she trust my judgment? Hadn't she come herself to ask for it?

" 'The trouble is,' she replied, 'that some of your good friends have advised me not to put too much stock in what you say. They say that if it's a girl who asks your opinion and she's not an absolute horror, you are ready to gush all over her. Well, I want you to tell me only one thing. Do you actually believe that I should continue to paint, or should I turn to some other sort of work?'

" 'In my opinion, no matter how difficult it is for you, you must continue to paint,' I answered at once."

Part of Rivera's artistic legacy was in recognizing and helping Frida realize her talent. Larger than life and surrounded by legend, Diego Rivera had shown his genius early, at three, by painting a train with remarkable perspective. Having received the best art training Mexico had to offer and having won major national prizes, in 1907, the year Frida was born, Rivera left for France to study European masters. He stayed there for fifteen years. By the time he returned, he knew he wanted to create art for the masses, and the first commission he received was at the Preparatoria, in 1922.

Frida should have rejoiced at Rivera's words of encouragement, but she didn't even thank him, only asked another favor. Would he look at her other paintings at her house on Sunday? When she gave him the address and her name, Diego immediately remembered where he'd heard it before. The principal of the Preparatoria was a good friend of his, and it had been five years ago that the man had complained about incorrigible Frida Kahlo.

Suddenly Diego remembered something else. This was the girl who had played games with his lady friends. As Diego was about to say, "But you are . . . ," Frida read his mind and stopped him by saying imperiously, "That was a long time ago and has nothing to do with now." The last thing she wanted to be reminded of at this meeting was her childishness. She covered her nervousness by asking defiantly if he still wanted to come on Sunday. Diego did, and he accepted the invitation casually, fearing that if he was too enthusiastic, Frida might not want him at all.

Rivera's account of their meeting reveals how complicated Frida was. On the one hand, she was confident enough to bring her work to the most famous painter in Mexico. On the other hand, she wanted to make clear she painted just to make a living. She was no "art lover." She was ambitious and independent, but still she asked for help. All her life Frida enchanted and confused people with her dualities. She was meticulous and intellectual, but earthy and sensual; she was small, yet she was tough; she balanced her physical pain with a great sense of joy in life; and her beauty contrasted with her scarred body.

No one knows how accurate Rivera's story was, because the painter was notorious for his amazing tall tales that, like his art, shocked, awakened, and created wonder. Truth interested him more than facts, and what his account revealed was that he was, from the beginning, fascinated by Frida. It was one thing for Frida to dazzle young Alejandro, but attracting Rivera's wandering eye and heart was something else. At forty-two he was sophisticated, had been married twice, and probably had had numerous affairs. Despite his physical ugliness women were crazy about him because of his extraordinary sensitivity and the great pleasure he had in being with them.

What drew him to Frida was an untamed, unpredictable quality that matched his own wish to surprise people. Frida was full of surprises, and the first Sunday Diego came to see her in Coyoacan, she did not disappoint him. He had no trouble finding the imposing Kahlo home on the corner of Londres and Allende streets. He knocked on the door expecting Frida to answer, which she did, though not from the doorway.

Perched in an orange tree, the same tree that appears in *My Grandparents, My Parents, and I,* Frida whistled "The Internationale," the Communist anthem, to her startled visitor. As she started to climb down, wearing worker overalls, the correct political dress for a young proletarian, Diego offered his hand, which she took, laughing at his bewildered face.

Frida held his hand as she led him into the house. It was quiet and seemed empty, which was just as well, because if anyone from her family had seen Frida with Diego, they might have been alarmed. They made an amazing pair, he at three hundred pounds and over six feet, she at one hundred pounds and slightly over five feet. She was delicately featured, he had bug eyes, full lips, and a lumpy face.

When they reached Frida's room, she took out all her paintings and lined them up in front of Diego. As he had seen with the three paintings she had already shown

him, her sense of form and color were exceptional, but
the portraits of herself were the most original and powerful of all her work. Rivera said later, "These [her paint-
ings], her room, her sparkling presence, filled me with
a wonderful joy.

"I did not know it then, but Frida had already become
the most important fact in my life. And she would continue to be, up to the moment she died, twenty-seven
[it was actually twenty-six] years later."

A few days after this visit, Frida called on Diego at the
Ministry of Education again, this time wearing jeans and
a black shirt with an enamel pin bearing a hammer and
sickle. Enchanted, Diego kissed her. No longer his wife
but still possessive, Lupe Marin was jealous of Frida,
though at first she couldn't believe Diego was serious
about her. But one day Diego took Lupe to Frida's
house, and she saw that the "youngster drank tequila
like a real mariachi." It was obvious that Diego was in
love with Frida, who was no longer the schoolgirl Lupe
remembered.

Frida was enchanted, too, not only with her *cuatacho*
(big pal), as she called him, but with the murals he had
been working on for five years. Begun in 1923, after his
mural at the Preparatoria, this was Rivera's first successful effort at creating native art. The Ministry of Education
provided a magnificent space for his tremendous theme:
the Indians, and the Indian part in every Mexican, and
their great struggle for justice. The building was three
stories high and, like many colonial buildings, surrounded a courtyard. On those walls he painted Indians
teaching one another in an outdoor classroom and divid-
ing the lands returned to them after the Revolution.

The Indians were Rivera's creation: they were deep

brown, round, solid, part of the earth. In those murals Frida saw Diego's dreams for a new Mexico, and she wanted to be part of them. She began to braid her hair with bright ribbons, and to wear long, colorful cotton skirts and embroidered blouses, the clothes of the powerful Indian Tehuanatepec women. Not only beautiful and symbolic, this costume artfully concealed Frida's injured leg.

Perhaps because Rivera knew that Frida was changing and would never again look the way she did when he first met her, he preserved her revolutionary, tomboyish dress in *The Ballad of the Proletarian Revolution*, his last mural series at the Ministry of Education. Diego painted Frida as a weapons courier holding knives in one hand and a rifle in the other, dressed severely in dark pants and work shirt emblazoned with the Communist star. Despite her serious expression and the exalted theme of her portrait, its creation was done in a different spirit. One day Diego looked up from the sketch he was drawing of Frida and announced solemnly, "You have a dog face."

"And you have the face of a frog!" she shot back, laughing. Besides calling him Carascapo (frog face), she called him Panzas (fat belly), and Dieguito (Little Diego). For a man who commanded great respect, even worship among his students, Frida's audacity refreshed him. With her he didn't have to be "Maestro," he could be Dieguito, a little boy.

With Diego painting from nine in the morning until nine at night and sometimes painting until morning, Frida learned strict work habits as well as technique. She began to paint more, believing Diego was the world's best artist and valuing his opinion as if no one in the world could advise her better. But Diego was a wise teacher and knew that Frida's imitation of his work, or anyone else's for that matter, would serve no one. When Frida told him she'd like to paint frescoes, he didn't encourage her. "Your will must bring you to your own expression," he told her.

Although Diego did not teach Frida formally, his work provided her with a model. She saw the richness of his color and the greatness of his themes and almost unconsciously began to absorb his indirect lessons into her art. *The Bus*, painted in 1929, looks nothing like something Rivera would have painted, but his influence is there. Just as he painted different aspects of society in a huge mural, on a small canvas Frida lined up an ordinary housewife, a worker in overalls, a child looking out the window at the land, a capitalist holding a bag of money, and a constrained European-type woman, all sitting next to one another on the bus. This was Mexican society in miniature. In the center an Indian woman in a large shawl cradling her baby dominates the picture. She is barefoot, a Rivera characteristic for the peasant. The style is primitive, flat, and simple. In one way Frida had a head start over Diego, because she didn't need to unlearn European style in order to become a native painter. Naturally exuberant, she drew painstakingly but freely. Without worrying if her sense of color was amateur or unrefined, she boldly used the colors of her people, olive green, orange, and yellow, in *The Bus*.

The fact that Diego and Frida were in love was hardly a secret, and when Frida told a friend she was engaged, he said, "Marry him, because you will be the wife of

Diego Rivera, who is a genius." Frida's family didn't feel quite the same way. He may have been famous and rich, but they knew about his womanizing.

Frida said, "I fell in love with Diego, and my [parents] did not like this because Diego was a Communist and because they said that he looked like a fat, fat, fat Breughel [a Renaissance painter]. They said that it was like marriage between an elephant and a dove."

Even though Frida claimed both her parents opposed the marriage, it was more her mother than her father. Guillermo Kahlo didn't see Rivera as a villain nor Frida as an innocent victim of an old man's lust. At one point he approached Rivera and said, "I see you're interested in my daughter, eh?"

"Yes," Rivera answered. "Otherwise I would not be coming all the way out to Coyoacan to see her."

"She is a hidden devil," Kahlo said.

"I know it," replied Rivera.

"Well, I have done my duty," the father said, and left.

Guillermo Kahlo, an atheist, certainly had no problem with Rivera's Communism, a belief which teaches that religion is a drug for the masses that, in its insistence on the people accepting God's will, keeps them from demanding their rights. He also may have had practical reasons for accepting Diego as a son-in-law.

Frida described the Kahlo family as "sad," partially because of their finances. Diego was wealthy and known for his generosity. Not only would Frida have no financial worries with Diego, the whole family could lean on him. Kahlo also saw Frida as a person requiring special attention. He told Diego, "Notice that my daughter is a sick person and all her life will be sick; she is intelligent, but not pretty."

Only Frida's father attended the wedding, perhaps because there was a clash of wills. The Communist Diego would never be married in a church, and Frida's mother most likely could not accept a civil ceremony as a real wedding. Senor Kahlo had a great time, however, at this unconventional affair. In the middle of the ceremony, he stood up and declared, "Gentlemen, is it not true that we are playacting?"

Perhaps it was just as well that Frida's mother wasn't there to see her daughter marry not in a traditional white dress but in native clothes that Frida later claimed belonged to a maid. For their wedding picture Frida sat beside Diego, looking quite relaxed and unbridelike, legs crossed and smoking a cigarette. Looking pleased, Diego stood beside her, tremendous, holding in his hands a cowboy hat that, if placed on Frida's head, would have fallen to her shoulders.

My Grandparents, My Parents, and I (Family Tree). 1936. Oil and tempera on metal panel. 31 x 34 cm. (Collection, The Museum of Modern Art, New York.)

My Dress Hangs There. 1933. Oil/collage/masonite. 46 x 50 cm. (Estate of Dr. Leo Eloesser/courtesy of the Hoover Gallery.)

Escuincle Dog with Me. 1938. Oil on canvas. 71 x 52 cm.
(Private collection.)

Still Life: *Cuando te tengo a tí...* 1938. Oil on board. 55.9 x 35.6 cm. (Private collection.)

Roots. 1943. Oil on metal. 30.5 x 49.9 cm. (Private collection.)

The Two Fridas (Los Dos Fridas.) 1939. Oil on canvas. 173 x 173 cm.
(Courtesy of Museo de Arte Moderno, Mexico City.)

CHAPTER 5

Frida Kahlo
de Rivera

FRIDA not only loved Diego, she also loved her new life with "El Maestro." Wealthy art collectors, artists, and intellectuals filled their elegant house on the broad tree-lined Paseo de la Reforma in Mexico City. The street and its houses resembled Paris and the famous boulevard, Champs Elysées, in Paris. Like Frida, Diego was full of contradictions. Rivera might wear boots, carry a pistol, and paint the Communist hammer and sickle, but he lived in luxury. Suspicious of Rivera, the Communist party in Mexico disapproved of the work he did for capitalist art collectors in the United States and for the right-wing Mexican government. The party accused him of having mixed loyalties and suspected that his political gestures were merely intended to placate the masses.

One of Rivera's most famous paintings, part of the Ministry of Education murals, was called *Night of the Rich*. It showed John D. Rockefeller, Henry Ford, and J. P. Morgan, America's famous capitalist robber barons, greedily eating ticker tape, paper which streamed from a machine that kept a running account of the stock market. By hiring Rivera to paint murals glorifying Marxist ideals, the Mexican government appeared liberal and concerned about the people's causes, yet the Communist party believed this was all just for appearance' sake.

The Mexican Communists also didn't like Rivera's independence, especially in regard to Joseph Stalin, ruler of Russian Communism in 1929. Following the Russian Revolution in 1917, Stalin made his reputation as a brutal leader who was willing to enact almost any radical measure to reform Russia. Rivera was not pro-Stalinist enough for the Communist party, who called him a painter for millionaires and a government agent because he had friends outside the party. Because he was his own man and refused to let any group—or person— control him, they wanted him to resign. This rejection didn't necessarily mean he had made new friends on the other side. The Mexican government considered him an agent of the revolution, which was, in fact, closer to the truth than were the party's accusations.

Frida was so enraptured with Diego that she remained mostly uninterested in politics. She didn't even paint much, focusing instead on being a perfect wife. She possessed her childhood dream, the flesh-and-blood, larger-than-life Diego Rivera, and she couldn't have enough of him. Some would call her love an obsession.

Frida left her own studio to visit Diego while he worked, bringing him, as she had seen Lupe do, dinner in a basket covered with flowers. Since Diego often worked around the clock, Frida wouldn't see him unless she brought him dinner. Other distractions from her work were Diego's occasional physical collapses from exhaustion. Frida took him to a doctor and insisted that he follow the doctor's instructions regarding food and rest in the afternoon as well as a good night's sleep.

Diego's health and the party's attack on him absorbed Frida completely. She defended him against all enemies, and when the party forced him to resign, she resigned, too. She was barely a painter, no longer a Communist, essentially a wife. Yet there remained a part of her, just as there had been when she was a child, that burned for its own expression, and she was beginning to feel the difficulty of being married to such a powerful man. Much later in her life she would say, "I had two accidents. The first was a streetcar, the other was Diego." Diego was both her gift and her curse. His love for her was her single desire, yet the central part of his life was his art, and if Frida wanted to be with him, *she* had to enter *his* world. Ironically, if Diego had been as swept away by Frida as she wished, she may never have fulfilled her artistic promise. His pushing her away forced her to find fulfillment elsewhere, and she found it in her art.

The last thing Diego wanted was Frida's constant attention and dependence on him. His single-mindedness about his work may have distracted Frida from herself, but it was Diego who encouraged her to work. He appreciated her uniqueness and had faith that her art would reveal it. Both a positive and negative force, Diego would always be part of her work.

Toward the end of 1930 the San Francisco Stock Exchange Luncheon Club and the California School of Fine Arts commissioned Diego to paint murals, and he was only too eager to accept. He couldn't wait to get out of Mexico to stop the hounding of the political right and left. Fifteen years in Europe had awakened not only a love for his homeland but also a great exasperation with its politics. With characteristic contradiction, the nationalist longed to be away from Mexico again.

Rivera had another reason for wanting to go to America. He told a reporter in the United States that he had come as a "spy," to bring revolutionary art to a capitalist country. He wanted to prove that art could change sophisticated, wealthy people, not just the peasants. None of his American benefactors was frightened by his remarks, perhaps expecting to win him over to capitalism before he convinced them of the virtues of Communism.

Diego also believed in machines as the most important solution in freeing the people, and in the United States he could witness, firsthand, industrialization. Rivera thought that machines could raise the dignity of human beings by doing repetitious work that killed the spirit. Technology, which created such marvels as cars, bridges, and telephones, could make life better for everyone. Only a few could afford a handwoven carpet, but many could afford the same carpet made by machine. Diego believed art would persuade capitalists to make conveniences and comforts available to everyone, not just the rich.

Frida, who only five years before dreamed of seeing the world, was also eager to go to the United States. She called San Francisco "City of the World," and was ready to show the *gringos*—the Americans—what she and Diego were about.

Imogen Cunningham, a well-known San Francisco portrait photographer, wanted to photograph Diego

Rivera's beautiful young wife who wore native Mexican clothes. When Frida came to Cunningham's studio, the photographer was not disappointed; Frida wasn't classically beautiful, but at twenty-three she was exotic and original. Wearing her hair simply to show off long silver earrings and a large stone necklace, Frida had wrapped her shawl in a way that let her hands be free, the same method used by women soldiers when they fought in the Revolution.

Unlike earlier photographs, however, this was not a warrior Frida, but a Frida content in her new life. This new Frida was starting a fashion trend that was later copied in Europe and America. "Frida had an aesthetic attitude about her dress," a friend observed. "She was making a whole picture with colors and shapes." Frida herself had become a work of art.

No one in any city of the world, including style-conscious San Francisco, had ever seen anyone like Frida. When famed photographer Edward Weston, good friend of Tina Modotti, met the Riveras, he described Frida as a "little doll alongside Diego, but a doll in size only, for she is strong and quite beautiful, shows very little of her father's German blood. Dressed in native costume even to *huaraches* [sandals], she causes much excitement on the streets of San Francisco. People stop in their tracks to look in wonder."

Never made shy by attention, Frida walked up and down the hills of San Francisco in her full skirts with many petticoats underneath, her head held high, bearing almost a headdress of ribbons, braids, and bougainvillea, and wearing lots of jewelry both fine and cheap. After seeing Frida and Diego, who typically wore a cowboy hat, wide belt, and a holster with a gun as insurance against political enemies, a small boy who walked by asked, "Where is the circus?"

From Frida's point of view San Francisco was the circus. She wrote a friend, "The city and bay are overwhelming. What is especially fantastic is Chinatown. The Chinese are immensely pleasant and never in my life have I seen such beautiful children as the Chinese ones. Yes, they are really extraordinary. I would love to steal one so that you could see for yourself . . . it did make sense to come here, because it opened my eyes and I have seen an enormous number of new and beautiful things."

On the other hand, even though many of their new friends were charmed by Frida, she didn't think highly of American culture. She called America "Gringolandia" and wrote homesick letters to friends. "Work hard, kids, and make loads of pictures to sell to the gringos and earn plenty of pesos!!!!" In another letter she confided, "I don't particularly like the gringo people. They are boring and they all have faces like unbaked rolls (especially the old women)."

Part of Frida's unhappiness in San Francisco may have been as Mrs. Diego Rivera. In Mexico she was also Frida Kahlo, but in the United States she had no identity except as Rivera's wife. Although she enjoyed the compliments about her dazzling appearance, they weren't enough. Rivera was busy, and Frida was alone in a strange country. Her closest friend was Leo Eloesser, a surgeon she consulted about her injuries, and in whom she confided her emotional problems, too.

Being alone was painful to Frida, but it also was her strength. Twice before, her creative core had saved her:

first as a lonely child, and then again following her accident. In the six months Diego worked in San Francisco, Frida again spent most of her time at the easel.

She began by painting pictures of friends, but the portrait of Luther Burbank, painted in 1931, was her first painting that was not pure realism. Like its creator, the work contains duality and contradiction. Burbank revolutionized agriculture by pollinating different species of fruits and vegetables with one another to create new varieties. Frida drew Burbank as a hybrid, a half tree, half man, holding a plant with leaves three times the size of his head and the roots of the tree wrapping around a skeleton.

Frida Kahlo and Diego Rivera, Frida's wedding picture, also painted in 1931, was another picture of opposites, but one that was intensely personal. Before the invention of photography, couples customarily hired an artist to paint their wedding portrait. Traditionally the painting showed a serious-looking couple and a bird bearing a banner with an inscription of who the people were and the date of the marriage.

Frida and Diego's picture, which remains in San Francisco as part of its art museum's collection, borrowed this formula, but Frida made the painting distinctly hers. First, the inscription over her head: "Here you see us, me, Frieda Kahlo, with my beloved husband Diego Rivera. I painted these portraits in the beautiful city of San Francisco California for our friend Mr. Albert Bender, and it was in the month of April of the year 1931." The wealthy and influential art patron Albert Bender gave Frida her first commission. It was he who arranged to get the Riveras into the United States despite their Communist affiliation.

Even though Frida put her name first on the title and says, "Here you see us, me," she painted Diego as the artist and herself as the little wife. He holds the palette and brushes, Frida holds her shawl. He looks directly at the viewer, she gazes dreamily into space. They hold hands gently, tentatively, perhaps acknowledging that Frida already knew she couldn't hold on to Diego as tightly as she wanted. Everything about Diego is big, but the contrast between their feet is amazing—his are five times the size of hers—and it symbolizes the difference in their art. His art was large, vast, and public; hers was miniature, detailed, and personal.

When Diego finished his frescoes in June 1931, they eagerly returned home to Mexico to begin building their dream house. Frida wrote Dr. Eloesser how much better she felt at home, but she also told him: "Mexico is as always, disorganized and gone to the devil, the only thing that it retains is the immense beauty of the land and of the Indians. Each day the United States' ugliness steals away a piece of it, it is a sad thing but people must eat and it can't be helped that the big fish eats the little one." The stylistic influence of the United States was changing not only Mexico, but the world, and the "ugliness" Frida refers to were things such as boxy, graceless buildings that were inexpensive and quick to build, tasteless American food, and a worship of money. Frida and Diego returned to the "big fish" a few months later, in November 1931, because the Museum of Modern Art in New York was planning a large exhibit of Rivera's work. A great honor for a living artist, Diego naturally wanted to attend the opening of the show.

Already impressed by the energy and power of the United States, Diego was completely spellbound by New

York's skyscrapers, noise, and bustle. Frida's vision of
New York differed from Diego's, and she immediately
wrote Eloesser about her impressions: "These days have
been full of invitations to the houses of the 'right' people
and I am rather tired but this will be over soon and little
by little I will be able to go about doing what I please.
High society here turns me off and I feel a bit of rage
against all these rich guys here, since I have seen thousands of people in the most terrible misery without anything to eat and with no place to sleep, this is what has
most impressed me here, it is terrifying to see the rich
having parties day and night while thousands of people
are dying of hunger. . . .

"Although I am very interested in all the industrial
and mechanical development of the United States, I find
that Americans completely lack sensibility and good
taste. They live as if in an enormous chicken coop that
is dirty and uncomfortable. The houses look like bread
ovens and all the comfort that they talk about is a myth.
I don't know if I am mistaken but I'm only telling you
what I feel."

Frida always spoke her mind directly, and she may
not have considered whether her remarks to Dr. Eloesser
about his country might have offended him. Her reasons
for supporting Communism were personal, compassion-
ate, and simple: it was not right that some people had
so much more than others. What may have been at the
root of her discontent, however, was not only injustice
and ugliness, but the part she and Diego played in New
York.

As a student Frida had demanded equality for the people, but now she had become part of the elite crowd.
Although she railed against capitalist America to her

friends, she still enjoyed long lunches at the finest Manhattan restaurants topped off by seeing Marx Brothers movies. In 1931, during the Depression, one out of four Americans didn't have a job. Frida saw people standing in line for soup and bread, men in ties and jackets who sold apples in the street, but still she was reluctant to give up her position as a privileged person. One day, while Frida was staying at the Barbizon-Plaza in Manhattan, the elevator boy snubbed her because she didn't look like a "rich person." As she got out of the elevator, she smiled at the boy and said sweetly, "Son of a bitch. Is that the right word?"

Such moments amused Frida, but the best thing that happened to her in New York was meeting Lucienne Bloch, a young Swiss artist. Frida and Diego were at a party the "rich have, day and night," and as usual everyone wanted to talk to Diego. Lucienne, who was soon going to work with the architect Frank Lloyd Wright, sat next to Diego. She was fascinated by him, because she had never met an artist who thought machines were wonderful; most artists feared machines were dehumanizing and ugly.

As Diego spoke eloquently to Lucienne about the promise of the new industrial world, she paid attention to no one else in the room, except, she said, "Once in a while I saw this Frida Rivera with her one eyebrow that crossed her forehead and her beautiful jewelry, just giving me these dirty looks." By the end of dinner, Frida had had enough. Marching up to Lucienne, dark, diminutive, and pretty, Frida spat out, "I hate you!"

Lucienne was impressed. "This was my first contact with Frida and I loved her for it," she recalled later. Lucienne became Rivera's assistant, and once Frida understood that Lucienne had no interest in her husband, the two became good friends.

Frida was glad Lucienne came to the opening at the Museum of Modern Art on December 22, because she knew few of the hundreds of society people that filled the high-ceilinged reception room. But even Lucienne could provide little comfort to Frida at such a gathering of what she felt were vapid people. Nibbling hors d'oeuvres and sipping champagne, in their evening gowns and tuxedos, New York's elite stood admiring Rivera's work, which accused the rich of exploiting the poor. By contrast, in her Indian dress and native jewelry, Frida was a living representative of Diego's art and philosophy.

While the crowd surrounded Diego, wanting his opinion about everything, which he was glad to give, Frida was ignored. But years later, when Frida's art hung in the Museum of Modern Art next to Diego's and commanded even higher prices than his, perhaps some of those present at that opening in 1931 regretted not having spoken to the shy young woman at her husband's side.

CHAPTER 6

Miscarriage

MUCH as Frida longed to return to Mexico, Diego was growing more attached to America. The wealth of the country may have been unequal, but he enjoyed more freedom and support in the United States than in Mexico, and the longer he stayed, the more commissions he received. America was also pragmatic; even though the reigning economic system was capitalistic, the art world didn't pay much attention to Rivera's politics. When Edsel Ford contributed ten thousand dollars toward hiring Rivera to paint murals in Detroit celebrating American industry, the painter accepted enthusiastically, eager to observe, firsthand, the capital of the machine. Many things were already made by machine, but cars, most of which were manufactured only in Detroit, were the first mass-produced objects.

In addition to the automobile, Henry Ford invented production with an assembly line, the most efficient method of manufacture. The car represented American industry and technology, and Rivera believed it would liberate the worker.

Despite Detroit's industrial achievement, Frida and Diego quickly discovered its prejudice. By the time they arrived in Detroit, the Riveras were already disturbed by Hitler's recent rise to power, but the city did not share their concern. Frida had begun using her middle name only, Carmen, in order to dissociate herself from her German ethnicity. When she returned to "Frida," she dropped the *e*, which was the European spelling.

The Wardell Hotel, where Frida and Diego were staying, did not allow Jews as guests. Since both Diego and Frida had Jewish fathers, Diego announced that they would have to leave. The hotel, understanding the honor of having the great Diego Rivera as a guest, begged them to stay. It was also early 1932, the midst of the Depression, and the hotel was desperate for business. Diego replied they would not stay unless the hotel lifted their restriction, which the manager promised to do. Diego's protest was ironic considering that his patron, Edsel Ford, was the son of Henry Ford, a notorious anti-Semite. If Diego knew about Ford's prejudice, it didn't stop him from taking his money. He may have enjoyed Ford's ignorance in commissioning a partly Jewish artist to glorify America. Frida, who never shared Diego's rosy picture of the United States, wasn't surprised by the prejudice and hypocrisy they encountered in Detroit and considered the incident a bad joke.

Frida tried to wake people up to the events in Europe and to their own prejudices, and acting outrageously in Detroit helped defuse her anger. When she first arrived, a reporter asked if she also was an artist. She answered airily, "Yes, the greatest in the world." She spiced up boring tea parties with Detroit matrons by discussing the virtues of Communism. One night at dinner at Henry Ford's house, during a lull in conversation, Frida turned to the auto magnate and asked sweetly, "Mr. Ford, are you Jewish?" Frida had outdone herself in offending the establishment.

Nothing in "the shabby old village" she called Detroit pleased Frida. Virtually everyone she met was petty and prejudiced, the only food she could stand was applesauce, American cheese, and malted milk. She painted little and complained all the time. Diego was busy night and day, and Frida, distant from the people and land she loved, felt as though she had lost part of herself.

A month after their arrival, Frida discovered she was pregnant. It had been many years since she had proclaimed her youthful wish to bear Diego Rivera's child; she often referred to Diego as her big baby. Frida wasn't sure she still wanted a baby of her own. After seeing a doctor in Detroit, she wrote Dr. Eloesser of her doubts: "Given the state of my health, I thought that it would be better to abort, I told him [her doctor in Detroit]." He gave her a dose of medicine to take for five days to no avail, and then told her she should have the baby with a cesarean section.

Frida questioned Eloesser, "Do you think that it would be more dangerous to abort than to have a child? . . . I do not know why Dr. Pratt thinks that it would be better for me to have the child. You better than anyone know what condition I am in. In the first place with this heredity in my blood [probably epilepsy] I do not think that the child could come out very healthy. In the second place I am not strong and the pregnancy will weaken me more."

Diego's part in all this also worried Frida. Rivera had fathered three children in his earlier marriages and spent little time with them. He was too busy to be much of a companion, let alone help her with a baby. What Frida wanted, much more than a child, was Diego. She continued her letter to Eloesser: "I do not think that Diego would be very interested in having a child since what preoccupies him most is his work and he is absolutely right. From my point of view, I do not know whether it would be good or not to have a child, since Diego is continually traveling and for no reason would I want to leave him alone and stay behind in Mexico, there would only be difficulties and problems for both of us, don't you think?" Frida ended the letter to her friend by saying that if Eloesser thought it would be less dangerous for her to have the baby instead of an abortion, she would.

The letter was long and intimate, containing the voice of someone starved for a friend who understood her. She apologized to Eloesser for "bothering" him with her problems, but she explained that no one in her family was strong enough to help her with this. She told him that since the pregnancy she was sick all the time, and her spine and foot hurt. "Nevertheless I have the will to do many things and I never feel 'disappointed by life' as in Russian novels. I understand perfectly my situation and I am more or less happy, in the first place because I have Diego and my mother and father whom I love so much. I think that is enough and I don't ask miracles of life or anything close to it."

Frida may not have been asking for miracles, but something made her change her mind, and she decided against an abortion. Although she clearly understood the risk, and reason told her not to continue the pregnancy, the temptation of carrying a future "Dieguito" may have swayed her, and part of her longed for the experience of motherhood. Despite her disdain of the United States, she respected America for its high level of medical technology and expertise.

Now Frida hoped that American doctors could perform a miracle and help her have a child, though she didn't follow doctor's orders to eat well and rest. Diego, busy with his mural, had no time to amuse Frida, so when Lucienne Bloch stopped by for a few days on her way to Wisconsin, Diego wouldn't let her leave, begging her to stay and entertain Frida.

Lucienne agreed and spent the next five months with the Riveras. Diego wanted "Lustucru," as Frida affectionately called her friend, to urge Frida to rest and paint, but Frida had other plans. She was in love with cars and wanted to learn to drive. She told Lucienne she'd driven a few times in the car Henry Ford had given them and had already been in jail five times for killing pedestrians! Of course, this wasn't true, but Frida never did become a driver.

Lucienne persuaded Frida to paint occasionally while she worked on small figurines of glass. More focused on Lucienne's work than her own, Frida suggested to her that she work on bigger things, make larger art, and Lucienne found the advice helpful. It was June, and the apartment was oppressively hot, but Frida worked a little. She felt sick but tried to ignore the ominous symptoms. Lucienne worried that Frida didn't listen to the doctor or visit him enough. Maybe she didn't want a baby, after all.

On the night of July 4, Frida felt especially ill, but the

doctor came and assured her it was nothing to be alarmed about. She should rest more, he told her. During the night Frida awakened screaming. Diego came out of the room, pale and disheveled, and asked Lucienne to call the doctor. The ambulance arrived at six A.M.

Lucienne remembered the morning well, seeing Frida "in the agonies of birth. . . ." As the attendants at Henry Ford Hospital wheeled her down the halls on the stretcher, she looked up at the ceiling and saw brightly colored water and heat pipes. "Que precioso!" (How lovely!) she murmured to Lucienne and Diego.

Frida lost her baby and spent thirteen days in the hospital. Her body recovered from the loss of the child sooner than her spirit. She cried and said she wished she were dead. Diego felt helpless and was afraid of her despair, but Lucienne, knowing one of Frida's strengths was her great sense of humor, came one day to visit and told Frida she had received a telegram from Mrs. Henry Ford. Lucienne "read" the telegram, using language that Mrs. Ford not only disapproved of but probably could never imagine. At first Frida was puzzled. But when she caught on to what Lucienne was doing, her deep infectious laughter filled the room, and she seemed suddenly to remember how to enjoy life again.

Of all the painful and unflinching portraits Frida drew, the one event she could never express was her bus accident. The miscarriage, however, drove her to paint the experience of birth and unborn children. A couple of days afterward, she asked her doctor for a book that would show a baby in utero, but the doctor refused on the grounds it would upset her. He didn't know Frida had once aspired to medical school, and had always been fascinated by the working of the human body. The doctor also didn't know that Frida was a woman who never feared the truth, only evasion of it.

Diego found a medical book for her, from which she copied a male embryo, perhaps imagining it to be her unborn son. When she came home from the hospital, she wrote Eloesser of all that happened and how sad she felt. But she ended the letter cheerfully, assuring him that she was surviving, because one has no choice: "I have a cat's luck since I do not die so easily and that's always something."

Frida's despair enveloped her after the miscarriage. Nietzsche's words, "That which does not kill us makes us stronger," could have been Frida's credo. She struggled to recover and read and reread Walt Whitman's poetry for its affirmation of life: "I dote on myself, there is a lot of me and all so luscious." Unlike Whitman, however, Frida didn't sing of her strength but painted what nearly killed her. Like the bus accident the miscarriage made her a different woman.

Diego asked Lucienne to stay with them longer, to be company for his wife. Frida enjoyed her company but resisted Lucienne's urging her to paint. Like her father Frida was neat and craved order, but anything, like a friend dropping by, would distract her from working. Lucienne remembered, "By the time she must get into action, something always happens and she feels her day broken up." Frida decided to study biology, anatomy, and history, and she would teach Lucienne Spanish. They even bought a blackboard, though little came of their attempts to study.

Despite her lack of discipline, Frida began to paint, as though compelled by the loss of the baby, and she began to take herself seriously as an artist. Unlike Diego, who enjoyed painting with lots of people watching him up on the scaffold, Frida liked to paint privately, with no distractions. Even a fly on her arm could send her into a rage. During her year in Detroit, Frida painted four paintings that marked a turning point in her art.

At Diego's suggestion she had begun to paint on metal, in the style of Mexican folk art. Tin, usually from a roof, was cheaper than canvas and lasted longer than paper. One of the most popular forms of metal art was the *retablo,* or *ex-votos,* found on church walls.

Since colonial times, Mexicans had commemorated God's miraculous intervention at critical moments with these miniature paintings. Often no larger than a post card, the picture showed an accident or illness and the heavenly figure responsible for saving the subject from maiming or death. For example, a *retablo* might show a man's leg being bitten by a dog and in the upper right-hand corner, Jesus; a picture might have a bed in the center, with candles beside it to indicate a sick bed, and a saint hovering above. Like a fresco, the *retablo* tells a story without words, but it's very small. Usually the picture has some text that includes the name of the subject, the date of the accident, and the saint responsible for the miracle. The *retablo* is a thank-you note to God, an announcement to the community of the event, and a method of healing. Today many Mexican people no longer have a painting made, but photograph the person who survived and write the appropriate information beneath it.

The *retablo* is a way of closing the chapter on a critical event and continuing with life. Frida painted her own *retablo, Henry Ford Hospital,* to help her heal from her loss. Instead of religion, art became her comfort as it helped her confront and accept her life.

Beginning with *Henry Ford Hospital,* almost all her paintings were like *retablos,* intimate and specific, dramatic, and sometimes violent. In that painting Frida lies in an iron hospital bed that seems to be almost floating in space, which is probably how she felt in Detroit. Like the cold metal bed, the background of the city is filled with hard man-made objects. Frida is naked, lying in a pool of blood, and like most of her self-portraits, her face is expressionless except for one large tear. Frida thus contrasts a stoic face with the graphic illustration of pain, characterizing the face as a mask that hides one's inner anguish.

She holds red ribbons that resemble blood vessels or pipes such as the ones she noticed as she rode down the hospital corridor, and they connect to six objects, some obvious and some mysterious, all part of the miscarriage. A snail sits over Frida's head representing the length of time it took to miscarry. The clearest figure is a baby boy, sitting Buddha-like.

Next to the baby is a torso of a pregnant woman, and below the bed is a carefully drawn pelvis Frida copied from a medical book. There is also an ugly machinelike object in the picture, which may symbolize her being pregnant in Detroit, or a machine that causes terrible pain. Finally, a large purple orchid, copied from one Diego brought her in the hospital, lies by her feet.

Years later, after more miscarriages, Frida said, "My painting carries within it the message of pain. I lost three children . . . paintings substituted for all of this. I believe work is the best thing." Suffering is invisible. One doesn't bleed from anguish, yet Frida, with bloody images, had begun to paint real but unseen feelings. Diego called her new work, unlike anything she had ever done before, "agonized poetry."

Henry Ford Hospital is missing half of what is found in a traditional *retablo,* an expression of faith and gratitude. No guardian angel appears, because nothing saved Frida from losing her baby. The painting contains the horror of her loss without God's redemption, but she had found another source of strength. With the love of friends, she survived the miscarriage, and she learned she could create, not as a mother, but as an artist: for Frida her art and friends became her salvation.

CHAPTER 7

Paint Your
Own Life

DIEGO and Lucienne watched Frida carefully, seeing her spirits lift when she worked, especially when she painted what she cared about most. "Paint your own life," Diego told her, suggesting she mark the events of her life with a series of paintings. She took his advice; though Frida's world included politics, friends, family, and of course, Diego, most of her two hundred paintings were about herself.

"I paint myself because I am so often alone," Frida once explained, "because I am the subject I know best." In the self-portraits Frida offers the viewer an intimate glimpse of herself, giving nothing more nor less than her own truth. She uncovered, through her art, the fears and sadness she hid in person, and like the *retablo* her paintings made her nightmares public. Because only she truly understood what her self-portraits meant to her, she couldn't understand why a collector might want one.

The work was by her, about her, and for her. What meaning could it have for anyone else?

If Frida's art, however, had been only about her difficult life, it would have been personally therapeutic but would have had little meaning for anyone else; few of us enjoy hearing about other people's problems. But Frida intuitively knew and acted upon what Ralph Waldo Emerson, the nineteenth-century American philosopher, proclaimed: "To believe your own thought, to believe that what is true for you in your private heart is true for all men—that is genius."

In life and art Frida was direct and concrete. She didn't try to represent the whole world in her paintings, only her reality, which was revolutionary, especially for a woman. The pain of childbirth, the sorrow of barrenness, the emptiness of abortion, were not appropriate subjects for art or discussion until Frida Kahlo began painting about them. The uniqueness of her work derived from the strength of her intellectual independence, her adaptation of folk art, and her openness.

In her work Frida used physical pain as a metaphor for emotional anguish. The accident did, however, cause deterioration of her bones and chronic discomfort, which she tried to hide from everyone. She always looked beautiful, even when she painted; instead of wearing a work shirt or smock, she wore her long skirts and embroidered blouses. She didn't complain, she didn't limp, and no one knew what it cost her emotionally to appear whole instead of broken. Only in her paintings did she reveal her suffering.

Frida's year in Detroit may have been miserable between being homesick and the miscarriage, but it turned her into a serious painter. Unlike Diego, who whipped out two or three watercolors a day, Frida painted slowly but felt her small paintings, few of which were larger than twelve by fifteen inches, were well executed.

Proud of her long work days, Frida wrote Lucienne, who had gone home for a visit, "I finished the last painting and I have been working six hours a day (very strange)." She then went on, "I am bored about 10 hours a day, and only if you come back will it be different." She signed the letter, "Frieda, Coocoo the Parrot Girl!" Her reference to the parrot may have revealed her longing to be back where parrots and parrot girls thrive—in Mexico.

When a reporter from a Detroit paper came to interview Frida because she was Diego Rivera's wife, the journalist became victim to her new self-esteem and her pleasure in shocking certain Americans. The reporter asked her about her training, and she replied, "No, I don't study with Diego. I didn't study with anyone. I just started to paint." Frida didn't crack a smile, but her eyes gleamed. "Of course, he does pretty well for a little boy, but it is I who am the big artist." Frida finished her speech with an explosion of laughter. Joking allowed her to deal with being ignored, the months spent in ugly "Gringolandia," and loneliness.

When Lucienne returned, she and Frida wandered the streets of Detroit, especially the poorer sections, which they found emotionally richer than the fancy neighborhoods. One day, on an errand to find sheet metal for more paintings, they walked past a long-closed store that displayed street decorations. Statues of a roaring lion, a white horse, and George Washington, surrounded by red, white, and blue, had once been part of a Fourth of

July celebration. Like the *retablo* or Judas figures, these humble and unpretentious decorations were not conscious efforts at art, but they spoke directly to the people. In *Showcase in Detroit,* Frida captured the universal thread of folk art. Festive, colorful, and upbeat, the painting declares its alliance with the poor, who are victims everywhere.

Immediately after finishing the store-window painting, Frida began a more ambitious painting full of outrage, loneliness, and her special mocking humor. *Self-Portrait on the Borderline between Mexico and the United States* is also done in a *retablo* style. The painting is called a self-portrait, but Frida is only one aspect of this complicated painting. Like a fresco, it can be "read" from left to right, beginning with the hot sun and the weak moon. Men are connected to the sun, women to the moon, and for Frida they represent a unity of opposites: light and dark, big and small, strong and weak, hot and cold, life and death, earth and heaven, day and night. Like Frida and Diego, opposites together make one.

The painting depicts Mexico on the left and the United States on the right. An Aztec pyramid contrasts with Detroit's smokestacks; plants and their roots reach into the earth while machines send their wires also into the earth, stretching threateningly over to the flowers. Rivera may have idolized the machine, but Frida despised it. A car nearly killed her, and it was in Detroit, the massive car factory, that she bled again in miscarriage.

Frida stands amidst all these conflicting images, herself in conflict. She wears a pretty pink dress, one she never would wear in real life but that she saw women at Detroit parties wear. She looks sweet in long white gloves, her face impassive as usual, but in one hand she holds a Mexican flag and in the other a cigarette.

In this painting the United States is home to money, pollution, machines, and pretense. Mexico is home to the natural world and Aztec beauty. The division is painted outside Frida, but in reality it existed within her as well. Frida was not purely Aztec; she was also European. She adored Lucienne, who was Swiss, and when she first met Diego, he wasn't speaking Spanish but French. Her closest friends were not Mexican, but European and American. With an elitist education she was not a peasant, though she sympathized with *la raza*. Capitalist money bought her the best medical care. Frida carried the conflict wherever she was, but it was easier to bear in Mexico, and she longed to go home. The painting was a cry to return to her homeland.

When she received a telegram that her mother was critically ill, she wanted to leave Detroit immediately and head for home. She demanded another despised machine, an airplane, to get her home right away, but no flights were available, and because there were tremendous rains in Mexico that summer, the Rio Grande had flooded, and phone lines were down. Frida couldn't even call her sisters, and she fumed at technology.

She and Lucienne took the first train south to Mexico. Frida cried most of the way, but for Lucienne the trip was enchanting, since it gave her a chance to see parts of the world she'd never seen. The best part was traveling through northern Mexico, where the vast desert, rimmed by the purple Sierra del Carmen Mountains, shone with the delicate colors of desert plants.

Lucienne couldn't console Frida on the long journey

because Frida wanted so desperately to see her mother. Although her feelings for her mother, whom she called "El Jefe" (the chief), had always been mixed, she couldn't bear the thought of losing her. She would never again have the chance to win her mother's love. When they arrived on September 8, 1932, Frida's reunion with her sisters was so emotional and chaotic that she and Lucienne forgot their suitcases on the train. But even in the tumult, Lucienne noticed how different the sisters were from Frida. Matilde's house, where they went upon arrival, was similar to their parents', with large stuffed furniture and shiny fabrics. Matilde dressed like a European, too. During their six-week visit Frida loved to make fun of her sister's taste. She would pick up a particularly ugly ashtray and exclaim, "It's so horrible it's beautiful!"

Matilde Kahlo was extremely ill, crying out but not wanting to talk to anyone. For a week she hovered between life and death, and when she finally died, Frida's sisters came to give her the news, all "wrapped in dark [shawls] and red in eyes," Lucienne remembered. "Frida sobbed and sobbed." Besides her own grief Frida worried about her father. He was lost without his wife and needed his favorite daughter near him, not far away in the United States. She and Lucienne took him for walks in the park, where long ago he had taught her to row.

Even though she dreaded her return to Detroit, Frida knew it was temporary, and she consoled herself with friends and family. Visiting the house she and Diego were building for themselves in San Angel, a small town near Mexico City, also cheered her. They had planned two separate houses connected by an outdoor bridge on the second floor. Designed by the artist Juan O'Gorman, the houses looked like two boxes, the larger one orange-pink, the smaller a deep blue. The pink house was Diego's, Frida's the blue.

A married couple living in separate houses was unusual, but for Frida, who liked quiet when she worked, and for Diego, who always liked an audience, the arrangement seemed perfect. The modern German Bauhaus style lent itself naturally to the intense Mexican colors and lush tropical landscape the Riveras intended for their home. Like Frida and Diego, the house, itself a work of art, blended Mexican and European influences.

Frida returned to Detroit in October, eager to see Diego but bereft from her mother's death and having to leave Mexico. She continued to bleed from the miscarriage, and the combination of losses made her especially needy of her "little boy," Diego. But when she arrived at the train station, she couldn't find her husband, until suddenly she heard a familiar voice call out, "It's me." She followed the voice to a wrinkled, frail-looking man wearing a suit several sizes too large for him. Frida squinted, and as the figure moved toward her, she recognized Diego—but a hundred pounds thinner! He had been dieting and working so hard, he weighed only 198 pounds.

Frida, who loved Diego's rotund, babylike body, worried about his weight loss. Besides looking ten years older, his skin was gray and his physical collapses became more frequent. He was working harder than ever to finish painting in Detroit, not to return to Mexico but to move to New York to begin what would become his most notorious project, a mural for Rockefeller Center.

With resignation Frida accompanied Diego to New

York in March 1933, glad to be reunited with Lucienne and Stephen Dimitroff, one of Diego's assistants, whom Lucienne had married a few months before. Together they went to Marx Brothers movies, ate exotic food in Chinatown that temporarily stopped her longing for quesadillas and pulque, and haunted five-and-dime stores for different things, including costume jewelry, which Frida made elegant when she wore it with her Tehuana clothes.

Frida spent more time with Lucienne and Stephen than with Diego, not only because they were her dear friends, but because the art world buzzed with rumors about Diego and the sculptor, Louise Nevelson. Frida knew Diego's weakness for women only too well, but she probably hoped her love would cure him of wandering.

Lucienne tried to cheer Frida by getting her to work. Frida had little interest in painting, but after watching Lucienne work on a fresco one day, she decided to try one. This form of art requires working quickly on wet plaster, which absorbs the colors; frescoes do not chip, crack, or fade for many years. Frida made a small self-portrait, but because she was not a fast painter, she found the process frustrating. When Frida finished, she looked at it and decided her effort was wasted. Around the painting Frida wrote: "Oh! boy, Very Ugly, *No sirve*" (it doesn't work). Perhaps her rejection of her portrait was her anger at herself for not being enough for Diego. She threw the fresco down, creating a crack, and put it into the garbage. Lucienne, who didn't share Frida's opinion of the work, dug it out of the trash and took it home.

During the eight months Frida lived in New York, she painted only one work, *My Dress Hangs There,* an oil filled with hard, cold objects except for a delicate green Tehuana skirt and burgundy top. Although her face isn't in the picture, it is still a kind of self-portrait, with the dress standing for Frida surrounded by alien things from North America: a toilet and a trophy on pedestals to show the American passion for hygiene and competition, smokestacks, an apartment building filled with apartments Frida called chicken coops. A prostitute and overflowing garbage added to the sense of decay of the city.

Controversy was beginning to surround Diego's work. Nelson Rockefeller, art collector and financier, had asked Rivera to paint a mural opposite the RCA Building in Rockefeller Center. Eager to accept the opportunity to have his work be part of a city that was the U.S. capital of finance and the arts, Rivera approved of Rockefeller's theme: "Men at the Crossroads looking with Hope and High Vision to the Choosing of a New and Better Future." Diego was on the scaffold fifteen hours a day, happy to be watched by hundreds of New Yorkers daily. Frida also enjoyed visiting him but didn't like the beginning rumbles of criticism toward the project. At first she dismissed them as the usual high emotions Diego's work created, and furthermore, Frida was not surprised by what she saw as American hypocrisy. If Diego mingled with capitalists, he deserved whatever problems he got.

When two-thirds of the mural was finished, New York newspapers began to describe the work as "scenes of Communist activity" and John D. Rockefeller, Jr., archetypal capitalist, was paying the bills. The papers also reported that the main color of the mural was red, the

Communist color. Immediately Nelson Rockefeller increased the number of guards, many of whom harassed Rivera's assistants.

For all her spontaneity Frida rarely became upset about things, but she sensed this time there was going to be trouble. Diego wouldn't back down, and Rockefeller had power—it was his wall. When Diego included Lenin's face in the portrait, Rockefeller told him to remove it. Rivera said Lenin had to stay; he would compromise by adding Lincoln to the mural. A few days later, on May 9, Rockefeller ended the dispute by firing Rivera. Within the year the mural would be destroyed.

Many artists, including Frida, rose to Rivera's defense by picketing Rockefeller Center and Rockefeller's home carrying placards that demanded, "Save Rivera's painting!" As a gesture of solidarity, Frida stopped wearing Manhattan fashion and went back to Mexican clothes. Believing the Rockefellers were scared off by public reaction to the mural, she told a newspaper reporter, "The Rockefellers knew quite well the murals were to depict the revolutionary point of view—that they were going to be revolutionary paintings. They seemed very nice and understanding about it and always very interested, especially Mrs. Rockefeller." Frida rejoiced at the chance to be helpful to Diego, hoping she could be the most important woman in his life again.

Despite the cancellation of the mural, Diego was in no hurry to return to Mexico. Although this annoyed Frida, as long as she was with Diego, she could be patient. Besides, she sympathized with her husband, as she explained in a letter to Leo Eloesser: "In relation to Diego's work the people [in Mexico] always respond with obscenities and dirty tricks, and that is what makes him most desperate since he has only to arrive and they start attacking him in the newspapers, they have such envy for him that they would like to make him disappear as if by enchantment. On the other hand in Gringolandia it was different, even in the case of the Rockefellers, one could fight against them without being stabbed in the back." Still, by fall Frida and Diego fought all the time about returning to Mexico. During one of these arguments, Diego picked up one of his paintings of the Mexican desert and shouted, "I don't want to go back to that!" He had spent fifteen years in Paris and the life of an expatriate suited him. It was easier to be a passionate Mexican nationalist when he wasn't living there.

"*I* want to go back to that!" Frida yelled back. Suddenly Diego picked up a knife and cut the painting into pieces. Frida trembled but knew better than to try to stop him when he was enraged and with a knife in his hand. When he was finished, he stuffed the shreds of canvas into his pocket and walked out the door. Frida felt sick, taking Diego's violent behavior as an act of hatred toward Mexico and a rejection of her, too. It was she who was dragging Diego back to Mexico, and she feared what that might cost her.

CHAPTER 8

Murdered by Life

DIEGO was used to criticism, but the destruction of the mural wounded him deeply. Still, he made no move to return home, but instead busied himself painting a history of the United States, this time on movable panels, for the New Worker's School. Every commission he looked forward to was canceled after the firing. Diego had enemies in Mexico as well as the United States, but the rejection in New York hurt him the most, because he wanted to stay away from Mexico, and commissions gave him the excuse to stay.

As much as their friends loved Frida and Diego being in New York, they knew the Riveras belonged in Mexico. Louise Nevelson and a group of friends raised money for their boat ticket home at the end of 1933 and "saw to it that they left," Nevelson recalled.

Things grew worse, however, as soon as they returned to Mexico. Diego blamed Frida for taking him from New York. "It's going backward in time," he told her repeatedly. "The world revolution will happen in the industrial world. I wanted to give up our comforts at home and stay to fight the revolution." Frida didn't agree at all and told him she thought talk of "world revolution" was ridiculous, but she also had her doubts about anything being accomplished in Mexico.

Soon after their return Frida wrote Ella Wolfe, one of the New York group and wife of Bertram Wolfe, Diego's biographer, that she was not happy about returning to Mexico. Eager for the Wolfes to understand that she hadn't forced Diego to leave New York, Frida told her friend that Diego wasn't working and that he blamed her for it. Even though she knew that she had never intended to hurt him, Frida confided that she had suffered from his rejection of her. Describing her husband as growing "weaker and thinner" and "sad all the time," Frida wished she could give him her life to restore his health. The letter to Ella Wolfe reveals a frightened, lonely woman who longs for her friends who live far away.

Although Frida understood Diego's reluctance to come back to "these people down here who are so damned stupid and more uncomprehending than you can imagine," she wanted him to make Mexico his home again and get back to work. Until that happened, Frida wouldn't be able to think about her own painting. Nothing, including her family and the new house in San Angel, which was quickly becoming a center for artists and intellectuals, caught her from falling into despair as she saw her husband moving further from her.

Diego eventually regained his strength after a doctor told him to "reinflate" himself. As he gained weight, he began to work again and to look better, but his recovery didn't help Frida, because she knew she wasn't the reason for his renewed zest for life.

Furious with her, Diego had taken cruel revenge on Frida. While he had never been a faithful husband, he now started an affair with Frida's younger sister, Cristina. The extent of the affair is not known, or even, more importantly, how Cristina rationalized it. But it is clear that the two people closest to Frida had betrayed her. Diego had taken away Cristina, the one person Frida needed to console her.

"Murdered by life" was how Frida described herself after her return home. Frida had learned how to make herself a magnetic personality through her appearance and wit, but Diego's and Cristina's affair destroyed this part of herself. She cut off her hair and began to wear ordinary clothes; Diego's rejection had diminished her. *Self-Portrait with Curly Hair,* painted in 1935, reveals a shaken and sad Frida, with eyes about to drop tears. More than depressed, Frida was enraged at Diego for what he had done to her, but she didn't strike back, at least directly, as Diego had at her. Once again her creativity saved her by transforming her emotions into art. While grief provided the spur to work, what she created empowered and comforted her to go on living. Her paintings took the place of her imaginary friend. She could look at them and think, "Yes, that is exactly how I feel, that is who I am."

Frida painted nothing in 1934, perhaps because of the depression she was feeling over Diego's rejection. In 1935, she painted two pictures which expressed how she felt about the betrayal by Diego and Cristina. One was the self-portrait with short hair and the other, titled *A Few Small Nips,* was a gory oil on metal that looks like something out of a horror movie. Even the frame is splashed with blood. The idea for the picture came from a newspaper account of a murdered woman stabbed twenty times by her drunken boyfriend. When questioned, the man said he had only given the woman "a few small nips."

The bloody woman, lying naked on the bed, with one shoe on her right leg, Frida's injured limb, is a self-portrait of Frida's feelings. She had been emotionally mutilated by her husband and her sister, and if one bled from emotional trauma, this painting is what it would look like: all who knew the Riveras understood Frida's message. The painting literally shows what happened to two strangers, yet on another level it accuses Diego of an assault that cannot be seen. Grimly sarcastic in its juxtaposition of the murderer's words and the blood everywhere, the blackbird's spread wings remind the viewer of Frida's winglike eyebrows as the bird's beak holds the ironic message, *"Unos Cuantos Piquetitos!"* (A Few Small Nips).

Besides the emotional trauma of the affair, Frida struggled with the physical pain she kept well hidden. Her flamboyant clothes, her deep and frequent laugh at tragic as well as funny things, and her extraordinary vivacity distracted anyone near her from her handicap. At times she may have even fooled herself. But her shattered body gave her constant problems, and it is probably one of the reasons she painted so little when she first returned to Mexico. In 1934 she had her appendix removed, as well as another miscarriage, and the first of many operations on her right foot.

During this time Frida took an apartment in Mexico City. She continued to confide in Ella Wolfe, writing that while Diego's life was full, hers was "stupid" and "empty." She said she felt she wasn't worth "two cents" without him. She told Ella that she was totally alone, that she had no friends in Mexico and that her family was no help.

Just as Frida willed herself to survive after her accident, she was determined to do so again during Diego's affairs following the loss of her mother and second child. Her diary reveals that she recognized her gifts of humor and wit: "Nothing is worth more than laughter. It is strength to laugh and to abandon oneself, to be light."

Diego's infidelity forced Frida to accept that she would never completely possess him, and that she must continue with her own work, because in the end that might be all she'd have. When the affair between her husband and sister ended in 1935, she wrote Diego that she knew that all the "English teachers, gypsy models, and students interested in the 'art of painting' " meant nothing to him, and "that basically you and I love each other." Frida decided to forgive Cristina as well, and her sister became an intimate part of her life again. Cristina's children, Isolda and Antonio, saw so much of Frida, they felt as if they lived with her. A doting aunt, Frida bought them gifts and clothes, hungering for her own children and remembering well what it felt like to be a child.

Despite the emotional turmoil Frida suffered in her relationship with Diego, she loved the life they lived in San Angel. Artists, writers, movie stars, and politicians came from all over the world to see the Riveras. One guest remembered, "I came for lunch and a spider monkey promptly sat on my head and took the banana out of my hand." The pet monkey, Fulang-Chang, which means "any old monkey," sometimes jumped through an open window and stole fruit from the dining-room table or wrapped its tail around the neck of an unsuspecting guest. Frida loved taking visitors to the circus, movies, and boxing matches. Sometimes they all went dancing at working-class bars. Whether out of revenge or loneliness, Frida began to have affairs of her own, with both men and women. In the bohemian world that she and Diego inhabited, bisexuality was unexceptional, although most of Frida's extramarital affairs were with men.

One of the most remarkable people who entered Frida's life and with whom she had an affair was Leon Trotsky, friend of Lenin and spark of the 1917 Russian Revolution. A longtime friend of Rivera, Trotsky appealed to him for help when Stalin threw him out of the Soviet Union. Diego invited the seventy-four-year-old revolutionary and his wife to live in Coyoacan, in the Kahlo house, and they arrived in 1937. Frida's beauty enchanted Trotsky, who saw her as a heroine of the revolution: "The new workers also need what you offer," he wrote her. "There is an affinity between true art and revolution. You show the concept of man's psychological complexity with the force of passion and instinct." Although Frida left the room whenever Trotsky began theorizing about Communism, or when she wanted to smoke a cigarette and knew he didn't approve, she found his old-fashioned ways charming, and she couldn't resist the letters he inserted in books he lent her. Soon they were secretly meeting at Cristina's house. She painted *Self-Portrait Dedicated to Leon Trotsky* for him.

Trotsky was not the only one smitten with Frida. Isamu Noguchi, the sculptor, also visited San Angel in 1936 and fell in love with Frida and her art. Only the diminutive Noguchi's fear of being caught by Frida's huge husband interrupted their passionate affair.

Noguchi said, "Diego came by with a gun. He always
carried a gun. The second time he displayed his gun to
me was in the hospital. Frida was ill for some reason,
and I went there, and he showed me his gun and said:
'Next time I see you, I'm going to shoot you.' "

Noguchi understood Frida's physical limitations and
admired how she used them to her advantage. If she
couldn't travel much anymore, then she painted what
she saw around her every day. "She didn't want to be
seen as a sufferer," Noguchi remembered. Her work
astonished him for its force and freshness, but Frida's
unwillingness to take her work seriously and show it to
people convinced him that she viewed her pictures as a
"private diary. I'm sure she never intended for them to
be seen."

Still, being Diego Rivera's wife made it difficult for
her work to remain invisible, and many of their friends
privately thought that Frida was the true artist among
them. Stephen Dimitroff said, "I would say, 'What do
you think of Frida's work?' Something in each of us
would say Frida was *the* painter, a painter, a genius. We
knew her paintings would have a niche, they were gems,
so different from Diego's."

Frida's recovery from her operations and Diego's infidelity allowed her work to flourish. She painted *My
Grandparents, My Parents, and I* in 1936; it was the painting of a woman fully home again both in Mexico and
with herself. From 1937 to 1939 she painted over twenty
oils, all of which reveal Frida trying to understand herself. *Me and My Doll* shows Frida sitting on a cot, without
a blanket or pillow, next to a naked doll. Frida loved
dolls and kept a huge collection of them in her bedroom.
She sits rigidly, wearing plain Tehuana clothes, with her

hair severely pulled back, holding a cigarette. The doll and the cigarette are a reminder that the days of childhood are past for Frida, and she will never have her own children to relive that time.

The painting is full of emptiness, revealing Frida's barrenness, not only in regard to childbearing but also to Diego's rejection and perhaps her mother's earlier disapproval of her. In *Fulang-Chang and I*, Frida again reveals her longing for a child. The sweet-faced monkey is in front of her, and a pink ribbon winds around each of their necks. Frida and the monkey share the same open, curious gaze, and her hair and his fur are alike. Their similarities create the characteristic tension and discomfort of Frida's work.

Despite the quantity and power of her new work, Frida wrote Lucienne that she was "lazy as always." Unforgiving of herself, Frida confessed that she used her illness as an excuse not to work, that in fact she was passive, living "on the air." She had painted twelve pictures since her return from New York, describing them as "all small and unimportant," and believing that they were so personal they appealed only to herself. Nevertheless, she told Lucienne that she sent her recent work to the University gallery, "a small and rotten place," in Mexico City where the paintings had been well-received. Lucienne was pregnant and Frida closed the letter by asking Lucienne to make "some nice caresses on your own belly." Still aching to have children of her own, Frida thanked Lucienne for having this child to whom Frida would be godmother.

Despite her insecurities about her paintings, Diego continued to push Frida to paint and show her work.

One of the first serious admirers of her work outside her circle of friends was Edward G. Robinson, a film star famous for playing tough guys and gangsters. In real life Robinson was a cultured gentleman who collected art. He and his wife, Gladys, made a trip to Mexico to see Rivera's work, and while Frida entertained Mrs. Robinson on the roof terrace of the San Angel house, Diego showed Robinson twenty-eight of Frida's paintings that she had hidden away.

Robinson quickly bought four, including *Me and My Doll,* for two hundred dollars each. Frida usually didn't like collectors, having once announced, "I get on better with carpenters, shoemakers, etc. than with all that crowd of stupid, civilized chatterboxes, called cultivated people." This sale, however, not only shocked but delighted her as she discovered a new kind of power. Frida told Robinson, "This way I am going to be able to be free, I'll be able to travel and do what I want without asking Diego for money."

As a result of Frida's participation in the group show at the University gallery, she received a letter from Julien Levy, a New York art dealer, who wanted to have a show of Frida's work in October 1938. He requested thirty pieces of art from her, and though Frida worried she wouldn't have the work done in time, she accepted eagerly.

Years before she had written Dr. Eloesser that "the most important thing for everyone in Gringolandia is to have ambition, to succeed in becoming 'somebody,' and frankly, I no longer have even the least ambition to be anybody. I despise the conceit and being the grand *caca* [the big shot] does not interest me in any way." Frida didn't care about fame, but at thirty she had learned that being Diego Rivera's wife wasn't enough, and her art helped to make her more independent.

Diego had always championed Frida's work and wanted her to have the attention she deserved. He believed in her art, and he wanted to launch her on a life of her own. As her show drew near, he wrote Sam Lewisohn, a collector and friend in New York: "I recommend her to you, not as a husband but as an enthusiastic admirer of her work, acid and tender, hard as steel and delicate and fine as a butterfly's wing, loveable as a beautiful smile, and profound and cruel as the bitterness of life."

CHAPTER 9

Fridita the Grand Dragon

WHEN Frida returned to New York in September 1938, she arrived alone. If she missed Diego, she didn't show it. Despite her letter to Eloesser disdaining ambition, she enjoyed being an independent individual and an artist. People stopped to talk to her not because she was Rivera's wife but because she was the painter, Frida Kahlo.

Although she couldn't visit museums or barhop because of her deteriorating right foot, she loved sitting in the St. Moritz Hotel's café to watch people walk by. Nearby Central Park provided the perfect backdrop for a woman who found people and the natural world always more engrossing than the city.

Diego helped her make a guest list for the opening, and it included New York's most powerful people, including Nelson Rockefeller. Frida was worldly and ambitious enough not to hold a grudge, especially against important people. She also invited artist friends

such as Noguchi, Nevelson, Georgia O'Keeffe, and Alfred
Stieglitz.

On November 1, 1938, the Julien Levy Gallery was
filled with people, and Frida, dressed like a dazzling Tehuana, helped create the right mood of *la raza* in which
to view her pictures. When Frida decided to show her
work—twenty-five paintings were in the catalog—she
had no idea whether viewers would respond to paintings
she created from personal experiences and without an
audience in mind. Perhaps if she had cared more about
people's opinions, she never would have had the courage to reveal such intimate work. Diego understood better than she what her work offered when he wrote:
"And Frida is the unique example in the history of art
of someone who tore open the breast and heart in order
to speak the biological truth of what is felt within them.
She is the only woman to express in her work an art
of the feelings, functions, and the creative power of
woman."

The exhibition was amazing and a resounding success.
Some reviewers were horrified by paintings such as
Henry Ford Hospital, but most people felt that they were
viewing the work of a genius. *Time* magazine described
her work as the "playfully bloody fancy of an unsenti-
mental child." Half of Frida's pictures sold in the exhibition, and she was delighted.

In December, Diego wrote her, complaining that she
hadn't written for so long he was worried. Still, he was
proud of her triumph and urged her, "Fridita the Grand
Dragon," to "take from life all which she gives you,
whatever it may be, provided it is interesting and can
give you some pleasure." He signed the letter, "Your
Number One Toad-Frog, Diego."

Frida was about to experience another turning point in her life, and despite public protests the attention she was beginning to receive delighted her. Earlier in the year André Breton had visited the Riveras in San Angel. Breton, a poet, was the leader of the Surrealist movement, which included both literature and paintings. Surrealism took apparently unrelated objects and put them together to create a superrealism. In much the way a dream consists of something absurd such as a swimming pool full of whipped cream, the Surrealists supposedly allowed their minds to be free of reason's control, and to paint or write whatever popped into their heads.

Breton had come to Mexico to discover new forms of Surrealism. He suspected that the Mexican embrace of death, its ease with ghosts, and its exotic landscape would make the country rich for his pursuit. Unlike European thought, which had made reason and rational thinking more important than other realities, Mexico blended fact and fantasy gracefully.

The moment Frida heard Breton expounding his theories about art, she disliked him for being snobbish and pretentious. When he saw her work, however, his admiration of Frida became reverence: he felt he had discovered a genuine Surrealist. Frida objected to this label as much as she fought being called a Communist. She didn't want to be put into a group and have people imagine they knew her because she was a "Surrealist" or a "Communist." She was Frida Kahlo, no more, no less. "I'm not a Surrealist," she said. "I never painted dreams. I painted my own reality. The only thing I know is that I paint because I need to, and I paint always whatever passes through my head, without any other consideration."

Breton was undaunted, and in the New York exhibition catalog, he wrote: "My surprise and joy were unbounded when I discovered, on my arrival in Mexico, that her work had blossomed forth, in her latest paintings, into pure surreality, despite the fact that it had been conceived without any prior knowledge whatsoever of the ideas motivating the activities of my friends and myself." He described her work as "a ribbon around a bomb," and possessing "a drop of cruelty and humor."

When Breton offered her a show in Paris after the New York opening, Frida entered a higher rung in the art world, because Paris was the world's art capital. Frida hesitated about going to the show, because she didn't want to leave Diego for so long. She had also been sick in New York and feared the same thing happening so far from home.

Frida finally gave in to Diego's urging her to go. When interviewed in Paris, she spoke temperately about surrealism: "I don't know whether my paintings are Surrealist or not, but I do know that they are the frankest expressions of myself." The label did give her a unique identity in the art world. Mexico's "tres grandes," the big three, Rivera, Orozco, and Siquieros, had defined their country's art as muralist. Frida had no place in that movement, but by being grouped with artists such as Rousseau, Magritte, and Dali, she was identified as someone besides a Mexican artist. Frida differed from the European Surrealists, however, because she wasn't trying to create a particular style of art; rather, her fantasies emanated from being a woman, a victim, and a Mexican with Jewish-European blood. She painted both the exterior and the interior of herself and the world.

Frida wearing boy's suit and cap. Ca. 1924.
(Photo by Guillermo Kahlo/courtesy of Dr. Salomon Grimberg.)

Frieda and Diego Rivera. 1931. Oil on canvas. 100 x 78 cm.

(San Francisco Museum of Modern Art, Albert M. Bender Collection, gift of Albert M. Bender.)

Portrait of Dr. Leo
Eloesser. 1931. Oil on
board. 85.1 x 59.7 cm.
(Photo by Kevin Noble/
courtesy of Dr. Salomon
Grimberg.)

Lucienne Bloch, Ernest Bloch, Frida, Suzanne Bloch, and Diego at the
New Workers School.
(Photo by Stephen Pope Dimitroff/courtesy of Lucienne Bloch.)

Diego and Frida after Diego completed the last fresco panel at the New Workers School, December 3, 1933.

(Photo courtesy of Lucienne Bloch.)

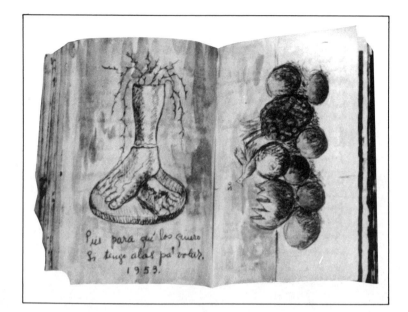

Frida's diary.
(Photo by David and Karen Crommie/courtesy of Dr. Salomon Grimberg.)

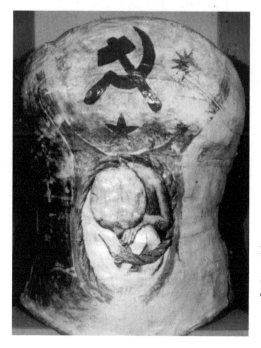

Frida's painted corset.
1950.
(Courtesy of Dr. Salomon
Grimberg.)

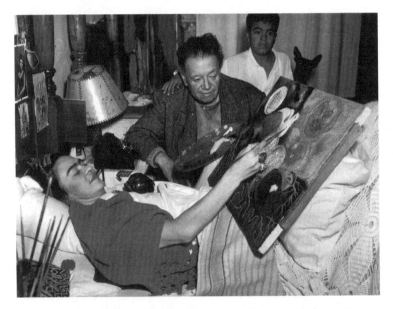

Frida painting *Naturaleza Vida* in bed with Diego beside her. 1952.
(Courtesy of Dr. Salomon Grimberg.)

Still Life: *Viva la Vida*. 1954. Oil on board. 52 x 72 cm.
(Photo by David Crommie/courtesy of Dr. Salomon Grimberg.)

Frida's last march protesting the United States' interference in Guatemalan elections. Mexico City, July, 1954.

(Courtesy of Dr. Salomon Grimberg.)

She arrived in Paris in January 1939, and judging by her letters to friends, she hated every minute of her three-month stay. She complained to her friend, photographer Nicholas Muray in New York, that Breton wanted to show her paintings with "lots of popular objects which he bought on the markets of Mexico—*all this junk*, can you beat that?" She was furious that an associate of Breton's, in reviewing Frida's paintings, told him "only *two* were possible to be shown, because the rest are too 'shocking' for the public!! I could kill that guy and eat him afterwards, but I am so sick and tired of the whole affair that I have decided to send every thing to hell, and scram from this rotten Paris before I get nuts myself."

Europe was in turmoil, and everyone was taking sides as Hitler began his world invasion. Although Frida cared about what was happening, the abstract theorizing by Parisian intellectuals bored her. She immediately became ill from eating French fruits and vegetables, and when she found out her exhibit was postponed, she lost her patience. She had allowed them to call her a Surrealist, she had to listen to politics all day, she was sick to her stomach, but she couldn't bear the idea that the whole catastrophe was to last longer than it was supposed to!

Frida found France to be a nation of Bretons, all "intellectual and rotten." She despised their posturing and longed to be home, where she would rather "sit on the floor in the market of Toluca and sell tortillas," than mingle with those who sat in cafés discussing "culture, art, and revolution." She saw them as parasites because they didn't work and depended on the gullible rich.

Frida's passion against the French made her letters sizzle. "Gee weez! It was worthwhile to come here only to see why Europe is rottening, why all these people—good for nothing—are the cause of all the Hitlers and Mussolinis. I bet you my life I will hate this place and its people as long as I live. There is something so false and unreal about them that they drive me nuts."

What disturbed Frida the most was how the French treated the Spanish refugees fleeing the Spanish Civil War. Spain was in the throes of a bloody conflict between supporters and opponents of the Loyalist General Francisco Franco. In 1939 Franco triumphed and set up a dictatorship. With the help of Diego, Frida helped to get four hundred refugees to Mexico. She wrote the Wolfes: "If you knew in what conditions those poor people who have succeeded in escaping from concentration camps exist it would break your heart. Manolo Martinez, the *companero* of Rebull [Daniel Rebull was one of the Spanish militiamen whom Frida met in Mexico in 1936 or 1937] has been around. He tells me that Rebull was the only one who had to stay on the other side since he could not leave his wife who was dying. Perhaps now that I am writing this to you they will have shot the poor man. These French mules behaved like hogs with all the refugees, they are a bunch of bastards of the worst kind that I have ever known. I am nauseated by all these rotten people in Europe—and these 'democracies' are not worth even a crumb."

While Frida fumed, she also made friends with artist Marcel Duchamp, who she proclaimed was "the only one among this rotten people who is a real guy." Despite Frida's loathing of Paris, the fashion capital of the world appreciated her style. Schiaparelli, the famous dress designer, created a robe inspired by Frida's Tehuana dress, and called it "Robe Madame Rivera." Unimpressed with French merchandise, Frida only bought two dolls for her growing collection at home.

Frida had to endure Paris until March 10, 1939, the opening of the exhibition. Breton did include other artists, most notably photographer Manuel Alvarez Bravo, as well as the "junk" Frida objected to in the show, but she was the featured artist with seventeen paintings. It was a terrible time for an exhibition, however, because the threat of war made art superfluous, and collectors weren't buying. People wanted to put their money into a bank, not invest in a painting. Breton's wife, Jacqueline, thought people didn't buy much not because of looming war but because the French were too chauvinistic and macho to be interested in a foreign woman's work.

Despite weak sales the art world responded enthusiastically. Frida wrote the Wolfes: "There were a lot of people on the day of the opening, great congratulations to the *'chicua'* [little girl], amongst them a big hug from Juan Miro and great praises for my painting from Kandinsky, congratulations from Picasso and Tanguy." Whatever doubts Frida may have had about her "small and unimportant" work appealing only to herself disappeared after the strong positive receptions at her exhibitions in New York and Paris.

The Louvre, the national art museum in France and one of the most prestigious in the world, bought *The Frame*, a self-portrait painted on glass with an exultant aluminum frame. The vibrant colors surrounding Frida's face and the yellow flowers adorning her hair give her a radiant, regal appearance. She had indeed become Fridita the Grand Dragon, and Diego was especially delighted that the Louvre bought Frida's painting before any other Latin American artist, including himself.

Pablo Picasso, a Spaniard by birth, not only fell under Frida's charismatic spell but also recognized her talent. A few years later, when he was standing with Diego in front of one of Frida's paintings, Picasso remarked, "Look at those eyes: neither you nor I are capable of anything like it." Picasso gave Frida a pair of earrings made of tortoiseshell and gold in the shape of two tiny hands, which she cherished, perhaps because they looked like her favorite flower found in the Mexican countryside, the *flor de manito,* a tiny flower shaped like a hand.

When Frida arrived home, triumphant, at the end of March, she should have felt her life was becoming fulfilled, but instead she found Diego again pulling away from her. By June 1939 they were separated. Diego said that divorce would help each of them to work better, and besides that, he wanted sexual freedom and knew his affairs hurt her. Diego wanted to be alone, he said, but perhaps he couldn't bear Frida's flirtations, despite his own bohemian views about marriage.

Frida said Diego's sloppiness and her penchant for organization bothered each of them about the other. She dressed up, put gold caps with rose diamonds on her incisors for a dazzling smile, and seemed very cheerful through the divorce. Both Frida and Diego made their divorce so civilized, it seemed a natural thing to do, and the former Riveras saw each other quite often. But friends observed Frida was drinking a bottle of brandy a day. She never wanted the separation from Diego, but her pride would not allow her to show it. Once again, as she had done when she found out about Cristina and Diego's affair, she cut her hair. Like Samson's, her hair represented power and strength, and in her case, sexual power as an expression of love. She felt angry and alone in her rejection, stripped of her sex, and therefore her power.

But Frida had discovered another power, perhaps more enduring, in her creative life. In the two years after the divorce, she painted more than at any other time in her life. She had already learned how to use her gift to bear her pain, and now, at the height of her creativity, she produced masterpieces. The combination of her success abroad and the divorce drove her to work hard to sell her paintings and not depend upon Diego for money. She kept a careful record of expenditures and income, but friends offered her money, knowing her graphic, intensely personal art was not easy to sell.

Almost all the paintings were self-portraits, and Frida's pain is so brutally exposed that the viewer struggles not to look away. In *Self-Portrait with Cropped Hair*, she sits in an oversized man's suit surrounded by her cut hair, which, like blood, represents her life. Her face with a man's haircut looks small, like a young boy's. In other paintings ribbons or necklaces wrap around her throat. They connect but also threaten strangulation, suggesting her efforts to ensnare friends and lovers with her charm. Being with Frida was like being with no one else. Her immediacy and intimacy made one feel as though there were no one else in the world for her, but this didn't seduce Diego. For him art always came first, love second. Frida couldn't have him. In fact, if he had allowed himself to be Frida's pet, it would have been her strangulation, too.

But Frida was lonely, and many of the paintings from that time have a monkey, cat, dog, or birds close to her, as though they were the only companions she could count on. They also represent the animal part of human beings, the part that needs companionship to survive, and the part that is wild.

During this time Frida painted the largest and best known of her work, *Los Dos Fridas* (The Two Fridas), remarkable for its mystery and beauty. Two Fridas sit, holding hands gently, perhaps the way Frida wished she could have with her imaginary friend. On the left is a Frida sitting erectly, wearing a high-necked Victorian dress. This is a demure and formal portrait, but the white dress is decorated not only with red flowers but with blood spots. Her heart is exposed, cut crosswise to reveal precisely its anatomy. The surgical scissors in her hand hold a dripping vein. Despite her hemorrhage there is strength in this woman. But the face reveals nothing, nor does the exposed heart. This was how Frida envisioned the European within her—stiff, mechanical, invulnerable.

Frida on the right wears Tehuana clothes, slouches, and holds a picture of Diego as a boy, a contrast to the other Frida holding scissors. This Frida's eyes are full of loss and pain, and she hides nothing. Stormy skies behind the figures suggest a feeling of despair. The painting reveals the split in Frida between the efficient and the mystical, the rational and the emotional, and the split in her country between the European and the Indian. The Tehuana is open, the European is closed, yet both Fridas are friends and comfort one another with their individual strengths. It would take every strength Frida possessed to get over Diego leaving her.

CHAPTER 10

The Blue House

IF FRIDA was trying to show Diego she could live easily without him, her efforts became meaningless in the middle of 1940, when Diego left Mexico and fled to San Francisco. A group of Stalinists, led by painter David Siquieros, had tried to assassinate Trotsky, and because Trotsky and Rivera had bitterly ended their friendship months before, Diego was one of the main suspects. Even in San Francisco, Diego didn't feel safe and carried pistols wherever he went.

Shortly after Diego arrived in San Francisco, Trotsky was assassinated at the orders of Stalin, and because Frida was an ally of Rivera, she was arrested for two days. Furious with Diego, she regretted the day he had ever brought Trotsky to Mexico. Her fragile spine was also making her life miserable. "Three months I was lying in an awful apparatus on my chin which made me suffer like hell," she wrote a friend.

When doctors in Mexico recommended another operation, Frida contemplated a trip to San Francisco to see

her good friend, Dr. Leo Eloesser. He encouraged Frida
to see him but not for medical reasons. With Diego
already working on a mural in San Francisco, Eloesser
seized the opportunity to play Cupid.

Eloesser knew how guilty Diego felt about the divorce,
and Frida's recent arrest disturbed him even more. He
spent hours talking to Eloesser about Frida's illness and
how Trotsky's murder had unnerved her. Believing that
each of them would be better off if they remarried,
Eloesser wrote Frida, "Diego loves you very much, and
you love him. It is also the case, and you know it better
than I, that besides you, he has two great loves—1)Paint-
ing 2)Women in general." Urging her to decide, he
warned that Diego would never be monogamous, but he
thought they could live together peacefully if she "sub-
merged" her jealousy through hard work.

Hoping Eloesser was right about a reconciliation, Frida
flew to San Francisco, where she was met by Diego and
Eloesser. She spent a month resting in the hospital, not
needing another operation, which was no surprise to
Eloesser, who suspected that Frida inflicted unnecessary
operations on herself. Some friends believed she tried to
hold on to Diego with her invalidism, thinking he
wouldn't leave her if she was a cripple. Yet Frida often
pushed aside her handicaps in order to work and when
she wanted to play. Sinking into a preoccupation with
her condition may have been a symptom of depression,
a cry for attention rather than a manipulation to possess
Diego. In one of her stronger moments, she asserted, "It
is preferable not to pay much attention to sickness,
because in any case one can kick the bucket simply by
stumbling."

Knowing Diego needed her boosted Frida's spirits, but

she wasn't entirely sure that she wanted a life with him anymore. Heinz Bergruen, a young art dealer with whom Frida was having an affair during the year of her divorce, said, "Her relationship with Diego was extremely difficult. Things didn't click anymore. She was deeply unhappy with him. On the other hand, she felt she needed someone strong to lean on. He was a heavy man physically; in a way he was a huge animal, and she was so fragile both physically and mentally. He gave her something solid to lean on."

Still, Frida was no longer entirely dependent upon him. She had grown stronger, independent, and confident. More realistic about what she could expect of Diego, she set new terms for a remarriage. Because she expected to paint enough to support herself, she would no longer depend upon him for money; each of them would pay half the household expenses. She also no longer wanted a physical relationship with him, because she couldn't bear the thought of sharing him with other women. Diego agreed, because, as he said, "I was so happy to have Frida back that I assented to everything."

Diego asked Frida several times to marry him before she accepted the proposal. His willingness to agree to her conditions convinced her that they could have a new life together. A few weeks before Christmas, 1940, in the city where Frida painted their wedding portrait, Frida and Diego were married for a second time, and this time it would be for life. In time they would regard the divorce as having been a necessary transition in their long, unusual, and tempestuous relationship. Although Frida knew she could never have as much of Diego as she wanted, she needed him less because her work had become central to her life. But Diego would always be the most important person in the world to her, and he, despite all his wives and lovers, knew that Frida was his true partner, the only one he ever asked for an opinion about his work.

Two weeks after the wedding, Frida happily returned to Mexico. While Diego remained in San Francisco to finish the mural, Frida readied her family's house in Coyoacan, her most rooted place, as the Riveras' new house. Her father had moved to an apartment a few blocks away. Diego would continue to use the San Angel house as his studio, while they began their second marriage in a new setting.

Frida prepared a bedroom for Diego she hoped would be so comfortable he would always return home to her. She also took such pains to make him happy because she knew, as she told Dr. Eloesser, that Diego would be "in a devilish bad humor until he acclimatizes himself once again to the rhythm of this country of craziness." A great big bed, the right size for Diego's girth, a rack for his hat and clothes, and a trunk furnished the room. Diego later added a picture of Frida over his bed and her letters under glass on the dresser. The room was off the dining room, where the Riveras always entertained. They never used the living room, preferring to sit around the dining-room table or outside on the patio. The living room became Frida's studio for several years, until she couldn't stand the coldness of the walls and floor in the winter. A few years later she and Diego designed a second floor that gave Frida a spacious, sunny studio overlooking the garden, as well as her own bedroom.

Frida changed the house dramatically, making it Mexican instead of European. Just as she turned herself into a work of art with clothes, jewelry, and makeup, she did the same with her house: its colors and objects were young and uninhibited, as though a much-loved child, secure and comfortable, had chosen her favorite colors and things, giving no thought to anyone else's opinion.

She painted the floors red, the walls yellow, with blue wainscoting. The outside of the house, painted in cobalt blue with red-brown trim, was just as colorful. The most striking house in Coyoacan, it became known in the community as the "Blue House." Frida explained the meaning of the colors in her diary:

GREEN: warm and good light

REDDISH PURPLE: Aztec. Old blood of prickly pear. The most alive and oldest.

BROWN: color of *mole* [chocolate-colored sauce served with chicken], of the leaf that goes. Earth.

YELLOW: madness, sickness, fear. Part of the sun and of joy.

COBALT BLUE: electricity and purity. Love.

BLACK: nothing is black, really *nothing.*

LEAF GREEN: leaves, sadness, science. The whole of Germany is this color.

GREENISH YELLOW: more madness and mystery. All the phantoms wear suits of this color . . . or at least underclothes.

DARK GREEN: color of bad news and good business.

NAVY BLUE: *distance.* Also tenderness can be of this blue.

MAGENTA: Blood? Well, who knows?

She painted her house in earthy colors, linking it to the natural world. Blue represented the sky and sea as well as love. *Petates,* woven straw mats used by peasants, replaced heavy Persian rugs, and upholstered furniture gave way to leather and wood. Giant Judas skeletons and devils greeted guests at the entrance to the house. Hundreds of puppets filled the stairway leading to her studio, and thousands of *retablos* covered the walls of the house. This collection was exceptionally extraordinary, because *retablos* were never for sale. When a grateful family commissioned one, it gave the painting to the church, which displayed it on a church wall. How Frida amassed the collection is anyone's guess, but she once horrified Trotsky by ripping a *retablo* off the wall and sticking it in her purse.

Despite her lapsed Catholicism, Frida admired the power of the *retablos.* Perhaps she wished that through art she could rid herself of her own pain, as the *retablos* helped families to recover from their trauma. If the *retablo* was offered to the church as a gift, Frida herself was the church to whom she offered her paintings as gifts to herself to heal her wounded body and spirit.

Anytime someone asked Frida what they could bring her, she always asked for a doll. She kept a huge assortment of dolls in her bedroom, including a special "doll" given to her by Leo Eloesser, a human fetus contained in a jar of formaldehyde. While some might find this disturbing, Frida treasured Eloesser's gift and kept it in a prominent spot sometimes in her bedroom and sometimes on a shelf in her studio. Not only would the embryo shock the more fainthearted guests, to Frida's great amusement, it also provided her with a realistic view of what her miscarried child looked like.

Babies and children, real or make-believe, obsessed her, and her nieces and nephews, as well as Diego's children by his second marriage, loved being around Frida for her playfulness, kindness, and generosity. Children connected her to her own sweet and sad childhood, to the babies she would never have, to her wish to mother and be mothered, and to the promise of every birth.

Moses, one of her most frescolike paintings in its detail, not its size, has in its center an anatomically correct fetus within a womb, flanked by a sperm and egg, and below it, the baby Moses in a basket. A giant sun radiates from the top of the picture, shining on what appears to be representatives of all civilizations. Frida used the baby to show how "everyone moves according to one law—life." Everyone is connected by the oneness of the universe, and the fetus represents the entire world. Juan O'Gorman, architect of the San Angel house, described *Moses* as "having so much in it you remember it as a great wall."

In February 1941 Diego returned home to Coyoacan with Emmy Lou Packard, one of his assistants and a friend of Frida and Diego's from their first trip to San Francisco. Because Frida was beginning to have to spend more and more time at home, she was delighted to have Emmy Lou keep her company. Emmy Lou stayed almost a year with them in a world that seemed like a fantasy. Although war was raging in Europe, life with the Riveras was peaceful, yet full.

Despite the war and increasing pain and immobility, Frida was enjoying life more than ever. After breakfast, during which Frida read him the newspaper to help protect his weak eyes, Diego went to San Angel to work, while Frida, when she felt well enough, went up to her new light, warm studio to paint. She could sit for only twenty-five minutes at a time, then she stood, stretched, and walked around a little before she lay down. After she rested, she returned to work. Perhaps signifying that she was taking her work more seriously than ever, Frida no longer painted in fancy dresses but worked in jeans and a workman's denim jacket. Sometimes Emmy Lou went off with Diego, other times she stayed with Frida.

At one-thirty or two Diego returned home and visited Frida's studio. He looked at her latest work and often told Emmy Lou, "She's a better painter than I am." Then they went downstairs and sat on the patio surrounded by the gigantic Judas figures and drank a few shots of tequila before lunch. Frida always made the dining-room table a feast for the eyes as well as for the stomach. She created a still life of plates, flowers in clay jars, goblets, and food. If Diego had been in the country, he brought Frida *flores de manito,* flowers resembling small hands, to adorn the table.

Although meals were usually simple, such as chicken with guacamole and tortillas, the atmosphere was rich with the excitement provided by guests and pets. Bonito, Frida's parrot and a subject in several paintings, loved butter. One afternoon he strode across the table to reach the butter, only to find that Diego had wedged it between a cup and a plate. Poor Bonito struggled mightily, providing amusement for his onlookers, who cheered him when he was finally successful.

After lunch Frida rested in a hammock on the patio or strolled through her garden, stopping in a small room she made into a meditation room with an Aztec offering altar. Since her return the garden had responded to her loving maternal care and had become a rich jungle of bougainvilleas, birds of paradise, and lilies, as well as turkeys, an eagle, a deer, monkeys, parrots, and dogs. "Animals, children, and flowers were Frida's main interests," Emmy Lou said.

Although Frida had a keen mind and sophisticated taste, she kept her fondness for simple things. When Diego had tickets for the symphony, Frida, who had no patience for classical music, sent Emmy Lou in her place, insisting that she wear one of Frida's Tehuana dresses for Diego's pleasure. Then Frida would go to a local *pulqueria,* a working-class bar, to listen to a mariachi band.

Frida's lighthearted days came to an end when her father died in December 1941. Characteristically Frida's health worsened with her sadness. The war, her father's death, and her pain put her in a paralysis of mourning. *Self-Portrait with Bonito* shows Frida in a dark blouse, an unusual shade for her, with Bonito, who had recently died, perched on her shoulder. With Frida wearing no jewelry or hair decoration in the painting, this is a portrait of sadness.

Diego's dreams of building a museum to display his tremendous collection of Aztec and Mayan art helped pull Frida out of her depression. Together they planned a museum that would look like an Aztec temple, and they were glad to build something at a time when it seemed the world was falling apart. Feeling close to Diego as she helped him with this project, Frida purchased a piece of land for him in the Pedregal section of Mexico City, an area dominated by lava beds. When volcanic rock begins to decompose, it is filled with nutrients, and on this rich, fertile land Frida and Diego planted a garden and brought their animals as they began construction. In its distance from world problems and its promise of their museum, the land became a second home to them.

Although Frida would never see the completion of the volcanic-rock building designed by Diego, she championed the project and pushed for its creation. In 1943 she asked the government for help in preserving the building after their deaths. Opened to the public in 1964, Anahuacualli resembles a great gray-black pyramid, and houses Diego's enormous collection of primitive sculptures. Inside, Diego used different stones to make pictures in the ceilings and floors. Tiny clay figures depicting ordinary life two thousand years ago, such as a mother washing her son's hair or giving birth, fill the museum, which looks as natural and unaffected as the art it contains. Although Frida didn't share Diego's passion for pre-Columbian art, the playful directness of the sculptures was similar to her doll and toy collection.

By the 1940s Frida was considered one of the great Mexican painters, even in her own country, which took longer than the rest of the world to recognize her genius. At the end of 1940, a Surrealist show in Mexico City of primarily French artists included Frida, and Mexico City's Museum of Modern Art bought *The Two Fridas*. In 1945 she won a five-thousand-peso prize at the national exhibition of the Palace of Fine Arts for *Moses*, and though she was in a cast from a recent operation, she attended the awards ceremony looking beautiful in a loose-fitting blouse.

Despite her fame she still vacillated between being Mrs. Diego Rivera and Frida Kahlo. As much as she loved painting, she needed prodding and spoke casually about her work. But when she let herself work, her paintings blazed with all that she kept silent about. Although she learned from Diego such things as skin tone and composition, she mostly gained inspiration from, as she put it, "the internal lyrical motives that impelled me to paint."

Her work revealed a quest to know herself and where she belonged. From her childhood Frida didn't fully belong in her middle-class pious family, nor did she fully belong in Mexico; her accident isolated her further. Then, when she married, Diego would not allow her to belong fully to him. Through her art Frida found her place: she "belonged" to her pain. It was uniquely hers, and it helped her to know who she was.

The backgrounds of Frida's paintings are like the background of one's life, giving clues about the person. Sometimes Frida painted herself as part of nature, sometimes as part of Mexico, other times with the mix of European and Indian cultures she possessed. In *Roots,* painted in 1943, Frida depicted herself on a *pedregal,* a lava bed, a seemingly barren landscape, but one that promises great fertility. Within this native background she feels most at home, and it is here she has planted herself. She has painted her own fecundity with plants and roots coming from her womb. If she cannot have children, she will be fertile through her imagination.

The painting shows that Frida has flowered in the desert, and it is into this dry earth she has sent forth her roots: she enriches the land, and it enriches her. Green leaves sprout from her body, sending out red blood-filled veins. Her hair is appropriately natural, hanging loosely, in this organic scene. The earth is dry, cracked with deep crevices, threatening to swallow her up. But Frida gazes out peacefully, relaxed, lying comfortably on what appears to be a hard bed of her own choosing.

CHAPTER 11

Los Fridos

THE WAR years became bearable for Frida when a new art school, opened in 1942 by the Ministry of Education, asked her, along with Diego and other well-known artists, to be members of the faculty. Nicknamed the Esmeralda (emerald) because it was on a street of that name, the school offered teenagers a chance to learn painting and sculpture, not necessarily to become professional artists, but to learn how creativity enriches one's life. Many of the students, ranging in age from fourteen to nineteen, came from working-class families with no higher expectations than to become skilled laborers.

In her role as teacher, Frida combined her tenderness for the young with her expertise and love for painting. Because she loved surprise, her classes were never boring, and her students, now in their sixties, poignantly remember their time with Frida. At fourteen Arturo Bustos came to the new school nervous, not knowing what to expect. He entered a large classroom with two different classes in session. As he joined the class in which he had enrolled, his eyes were drawn to the other teacher in the room, Frida Kahlo. She was "amazing looking," he recalled. "She not only made art, she herself was a work of art." Arturo immediately switched into Frida's classes.

Frida smiled at her students and said in a conspiratorial tone, "Okay, youngsters, let's work. I will be kind of your teacher; I am not really that. I only want to be your friend. I have never been an art teacher, and I don't believe I ever will be, because I am always learning."

Guillermo Monroy, another student, could scarcely concentrate on her words because he was fascinated by "her eyebrows, which were like the delicate wings of a bird," her frequent smile, which made her red lips look like flowers, and the black *rebozo* decorated with green leaves that rested easily on her shoulders. "Frida was there, in front of us, amazingly calm. Her hands, one on top of the other, were curled and elegant with perfectly manicured nails shining red and brilliant. She stood before us like a bouquet of stupendous flowers."

"La Maestra" went on with her introduction to the class, saying, "Certainly, painting is the greatest there is, but to do it well is very difficult. It is necessary to learn very well the craft, to have strong discipline, and above all, to have love, to feel a great love for painting. Once and for all, I am going to tell you that, if the little experience that I have as a painter helps you some, you will tell me and with me you will paint all that you love and feel. I will teach you the best I can. From time to time I will permit myself to make some observations about your work, but also I ask you, as pals that we already are, that when I show you my work you will do the same.

"I will never remove a pencil or brush to correct you; I want you to know, dear children, there doesn't exist a single teacher in the land who knows how to teach art. This is truly impossible. We will talk much, certainly, of the different techniques that one employs in the plastic arts, of the form and content in art and of all those things that are intimately related with our work. I hope that you won't be bored with me and, when I displease you, I request, please, that you not be silent, okay?"

None of the students had ever seen or heard a teacher like this. Besides being beautiful and kindhearted, Frida was famous, too. She didn't simply want to teach the young people to paint, she wanted to teach them how to live life. Young and impressionable, their way of seeing was changed by Frida, and in their old age her students still speak of her as their greatest *maestra*. On Fridays she took them to the market where everything, from live chickens to puppets, were sold. She would buy tacos for her students and exclaim, *"Tacos! Tacos indigineas!"* For Frida tacos were native culture, and she wanted her class to love *la raza* and Mexico—in other words, to love themselves. Along the way to the market, she taught them songs and told them, "Here life is hard, but tasty."

"She took us to the markets, the factories, the countryside, where we mixed with the people," Guillermo Monroy said. "And we actively participated in public demonstrations to fight political and social injustice. Frida told us that the direct contact with life would open our horizons and enrich our aesthetic and humane sensibilities."

Frida also wanted them to see their surroundings and their own lives clearly. Sitting on the floor in front of them one day, she asked them to sit around her and listen carefully: "Don't copy anymore. Paint your houses, your brothers and sisters, the bus, that which you pass by. Paint what you want." Then she took out marbles and tops, and played with them, making good her promise that she wanted, most of all, to be their friend.

Frida also wanted to teach her students about the power of art in making people aware of other lives and of beauty and suffering outside themselves. Besides taking her students to the park and the streets to observe life, she encouraged them to become students of art, and she brought them examples of many artists' work. Picasso and the naturalist Rousseau, whose influence shows in Frida's work, were among her favorites. She also trained them in the way she trained herself, by looking at books with detailed botanical and biological drawings.

Even though her students were young, they were sensitive to Frida's physical limitations. When after a few months she told them she no longer could travel to Mexico City to teach, they were disappointed but not surprised. Frida, however, didn't want to stop teaching, so she invited the class to Coyoacan, to paint in her garden. Most of the students enrolled in other classes because they were unwilling or unable to travel to the Blue House. But four were committed to studying with Frida: Arturo Garcia Bustos, Guillermo Monroy, Arturo Estrada, and Fanny Rabel. They would work with her for three years, and as their devotion grew, classmates began to call them Los Fridos, a name they took as a compliment

and adopted proudly. From the first day Frida opened
her house to them and told them the garden was theirs,
she declared them family and part of her life.

The four teenagers immediately were absorbed by Frida's magic. They worked in the garden while she worked
alone in her studio. After a few hours she came outside
with food and drink for the class, and at the end of the
day sometimes they went to the movies. The pleasure
of the movie was secondary to the thrill of going out
with their beautiful, adored Frida. Remembering the
purple *rebozo* she wore when she took him to the movies, Arturo Bustos admitted, "We were all in love with
Frida."

Frida rested often, and many mornings the Fridos
found their teacher in bed, not in her studio. When she
was wearing a plaster cast on her upper torso, she tried
to make light of it by having her students paint it or buy
"cockamamies," tatoolike decals to decorate the cast. On
one corset Frida painted a hammer and sickle with an
embryo beneath it. Frida loathed the casts, which were
hot, restricted her movement, and made clothes difficult
to wear. But without them she was in constant pain and
couldn't work at all.

Frida occasionally called the Fridos upstairs to show
them what she was working on. When she was painting
The Broken Column, one of her most disturbing works,
she taught the students a lesson in distinction. In the
picture Frida stands in the foreground with a lava bed,
similar to the one in *Roots*, behind her. Metal nails pierce
Frida's body and, where her spine should be, is an
exposed, broken Greek column. Her body is held
together by a steel surgical corset, but it doesn't repair

the broken spine. No blood or tears punctuate the drawing, but the nails, cracked spinal column, and corset expose her agony. Frida is naked from the waist up.

"At first I painted it all naked," Frida told them. "But then I covered the lower torso, not because I care about stupid rules about modesty. The nakedness distracted from the point of the painting, that's why I changed it," she explained.

Fanny Rabel, the only girl in the group, said, "Frida had a gift to fascinate people, an enormous love of life. Frida was a walking flower. She said, 'What's this thing of giving classes? I don't know. What's it about? You are one of my *muchachitas*.' Sometimes Frida was a big sister, other times a mother who watched her little ones. But she was always friendly and was equal with us. After a while it was as though we couldn't live without her."

One morning Frida, walking with her hair down and shining in the sun, heard singing in the garden. She stopped and found Guillermo Monroy painting a *maguey*, the squat, fleshy-leaved plant that *pulque* is made from. Frida quietly stood out of sight for a while, watching and listening. Then she met the boy's eyes and said, "Keep painting, Monroycito, give yourself pleasure with this maguey and keep singing. Don't ever stop singing." She gave him a kiss on the cheek and left.

The classes, always held in the garden, were filled with lots of talking, but without formal lessons. Time spent with Frida was more like a fiesta than school. Occasionally Diego came home for lunch and walked through the garden, making suggestions and explaining theories in contrast to Frida's instinctive, spontaneous teaching. One day the students arrived to find nothing especially set up for them to draw. "What should we draw?" they asked.

"Draw me!" Frida answered, laughing, hands on her hips. And they did. Like Frida they also drew inspiration from the birds and animals who lived in the garden. Each animal had a name and was loved like a child.

Diego and Frida both wanted the Fridos to have experience painting more than small canvases. In mid-1943 they obtained permission from the government to decorate La Rosita, a *pulqueria* a few blocks from the Blue House. Excited about reviving the custom of painting murals on the exterior walls of *pulquerias,* a form of art that had fallen into disuse, the Riveras supplied paint and brushes and supervised the work, though they didn't paint. The bar's name, the little rose, and its main drink, pulque, provided the theme for the murals, and each student interpreted the subjects freely. Fanny Rabel painted roses in a pasture.

The Fridos also used Frida and Diego as models for their figures, and in June they inaugurated the newly painted bar with a party attended by entertainers, famous friends of the Riveras, and politicians. Frida drank and sang and, despite her corset, danced. Guillermo Monroy wrote a song in honor of the occasion: "It took much work to paint La Rosita. The people had forgotten *pulqueria* art. Lady Frida de Rivera, our beloved teacher, told us: Come children, I will show you life. Friends of Coyoacan, if you want to have fun, La Rosita will give you pleasure. Look at how pretty she is!"

In 1945 the Fridos painted a *lavadoria,* a place used exclusively by poor women who washed other people's laundry. Before the government provided the building, these women washed clothes in the nearby river. This project merged perfectly the Communist ideals Frida had taught her students along with painting techniques. The paintings showed the women at work—washing, ironing, sewing—and relaxing at a meal after work. In gratitude the laundry women brought the artists food, and they all ate together.

"We worked very hard to please her," Arturo Bustos said. "Our affection for her drove us to make better art. She never criticized sharply, but she was clear about what was good and what wasn't." More than art lessons, Frida gave them confidence in themselves as she opened their eyes to the beauty of the world. She also sensitized them to Mexican mural art with its social messages. When the young people came to her, they felt they had to do political art or they wouldn't be accomplished. Frida understood their feelings, because she, too, thought her art should have a socialist message. She knew, however, that art could be about another form of tyranny, internal oppression.

When the Fridos graduated from the Esmeralda in 1945, Frida told them how sad she was that they would not be coming anymore, but none of them stayed away from her for long. She found jobs for them, lent them money, listened to their problems, and they visited her often for the rest of her life, even when it became painful to see her so deteriorated by pain and drugs. When Arturo Bustos grew up, he moved to Coyoacan, where he raised his family and painted murals. The village allowed him to feel close to the first woman he had loved. Bustos and his wife, Rina, who studied with Rivera, visit Frida's house often. Although the furniture and mementos remain, they say it is like an abandoned house without Frida. A death mask of her face and her ashes in the studio are a reminder that no one will ever again pick up the immaculate, orderly brushes beside Frida's easel. The *pulqueria* and *lavadoria* are no longer part of Coyoacan, but Arturo and Rina recently planted a public garden near the Blue House to remember the time when Frida was mother, sister, teacher, and friend to young artists.

CHAPTER 12

Tree of Hope, Hold Steady

"I AM not sick. I am broken. But I am happy to be alive as long as I can paint." By 1944 Frida could no longer hide her illness. Whether sitting, standing, or lying down, she was in constant pain, and the battle to keep her body from interfering with her life was exhausting. The streetcar accident had forced her to confront death, and she had even learned to laugh at it. But now, as she approached forty and her body was rapidly deteriorating, death felt too near and real.

In the last ten years of her life, Frida endured twenty-eight steel, plaster, or leather corsets, one of which required her to sit upright for three months. The corsets felt like punishment, but for what she didn't know. Ella Paresce, an American pianist who visited Frida often, remembered how one cast almost killed her. Frida had allowed a friend who happened to be a doctor, but with little experience in applying casts, to put a plaster corset on her one afternoon while friends were over. Everyone watched and laughed along with Frida as he molded it to her body.

"Then during the night," Ella explained, "the corset began to harden, as it was supposed to do. I happened to be spending the night there in the next room, and about half past four or five in the morning, I heard a crying, nearly shrieks. I jumped out of the bed and went in, and there was Frida saying she couldn't breathe! She couldn't breathe!

"The corset had hardened, but it hardened so much that it pressed her lungs. It made pleats all around her body. So I tried to get a doctor. Nobody would pay any attention at that hour in the morning, so finally I took a razor blade and knelt on the bed over Frida. I began slowly, slowly cutting that corset right over her breast. I made about a two-inch cut so that she could breathe, and then we waited until a doctor appeared, and he did all the rest. Afterward we laughed to tears over this thing."

As Frida began to feel her time shortening, she tightened her grasp on all that mattered to her. In rejecting her Catholic childhood, she looked for life's meaning in what she already knew and loved: painting, friends, family, Communism, and Diego all became acts of faith. Diego especially became important, because by keeping fresh her passion for him, she remembered the days of her relatively strong youth. As their relationship had moved beyond his being her husband and lover, she made him her little boy, the baby they never had. Diego enjoyed this role so much that when he, as an old man, painted the mural *Sunday Afternoon at Alameda Park*, he painted himself as a little boy holding the grown-up Frida's hand, as though she were his nanny or mother.

Although Frida included Diego in many paintings, she also wanted to capture him in words. In her "Portrait of Diego," written in 1949, she described her "difficult and obscure role of ally to an extraordinary being." Comparing herself to natural forces, she wrote, "But I do not believe that the banks of a river suffer for letting the water run, or that the earth suffers because it rains, the atom suffers discharging its energy . . ."

She believed in Diego's genius, his vision of the world, and valued his art as a way to awaken people. "Working always, Diego does not live a life one can call normal," Frida wrote. "His capacity for energy breaks clocks and calendars. He is the eternal curious one, the eternal conversationalist, the eternal painter. His diversion is his work, he hates galleries and finds wonder in truly popular fiestas." Frida may have written these words to downplay the high-society part of her husband that she disliked, or perhaps Frida, who sometimes painted a face that was half Diego, half Frida, was blurring the distinctions between them.

Despite Frida's decline she still could create the persona of a sexy, powerful, and fun-loving woman through her letters. To the Wolfes she wrote: "Do you still remember that here in Coyoacan there exists a very high-born lady, much esteemed by everyone, who is some . . . friend all right, and who is ever desirous of once again contemplating your beloved face in this lovely land called Tenochitlan?" Frida informed them she wore "a simple plaster, my spine still can resist a couple more blows." The Riveras were better than ever, she assured them; they were short on "dough," but they could still afford tequila, and she was a "teecher" (purposely misspelled in Spanish), which was a step up in status though it constrained her.

She also told them that Diego's daughter, Lupita, had moved in with them. "Said event turned me into an adopted 'mommy' with her adoptive child. I can't complain because the girl is good with Miguel Angel [an assistant in the house] and more or less has adapted to her daddy's character, but just the same, my life style is not very alluring, shall we say. Because since 1929 to the present 1944, I can't recall A SINGLE PERIOD OF TIME during which the Rivera marriage did not have AT LEAST ONE person in tandem and living in: home, sweet home!"

Frida told the Wolfes that she was drinking less by using her "iron will," and that binges were infrequent. Although Frida had always enjoyed alcohol, no one worried much about her excesses, because everyone knew her discipline and strong will. By the end of the war, however, Frida's pain was so severe and constant, she took to drinking a little all day long. Worse, she had become addicted to the painkillers given to her after her operations.

Of all her work, the diary she began in 1944 is the freest and most private in image and word. She often worked from the Surrealist technique of making an ink blot on the fold of the page and drawing something from the random, apparently meaningless, mark of ink. The creation of art from accident may have had special meaning for a woman whose art began from a bus accident. One such drawing in the diary is of a face, human on one side, animal on the other. Next to the portrait is

Frida, one-legged, on a pedestal with her head and hands falling off. "I am the disintegration" appears over her head. Both the drawings and writings display flashes of brilliance, but they also betray a mind clouded by pain and drugs. As her health left her, so did her hopeful, courageous spirit.

In 1950 Frida entered the English Hospital in Mexico City, not to return home for a year. In the quiet hospital, Frida made life fun, a fiesta, and just as in Coyoacan, she loved having visitors. Diego took a room next door and joined the party. Nurses and doctors peeked in to watch Laurel and Hardy and Charlie Chaplin movies on the screen and projector Diego brought in each week. Frida, hating the bland hospital food, insisted on tequila, enchiladas, and mole for all. Frida's sisters were always with her, and there were always different friends around. Her corset was like a guest book signed and decorated with photos and decals.

Lying flat on her back, Frida wore flowers in her hair, her face radiant with her expert use of makeup. Every finger glittered with a ring. Even so, all the fun and disguise couldn't hide the beginning of Frida's journey toward death. With her sad, frightened eyes sunk deep, and her face pale and lined, not even her powerful eyebrows and exotic mustache distracted her visitors' eyes from her suffering.

In her confinement Frida's need for attention and connection to people grew even stronger. She entertained friends with stories about her father and Diego and offered opinions about everything, including medicine, politics, sex, free love, and the evils of Catholicism. Friends who had come to cheer her left feeling comforted by her interest in them. "We all needed her,"

Fanny Rabel remembered. "She did not concentrate on herself. She was full of interest in others and the outside world. She would say, 'Tell me things. Tell me about your childhood.' Frida said that she liked this better than the movies. She would become very moved, and sometimes she cried when people talked. She could listen for hours."

Sugar skulls, wax doves, candelabra, books, and a Russian flag made the usually impersonal hospital room uniquely Frida's. Her carefully organized paints and brushes were beside the bed, but for months she couldn't paint, and she was desperate with frustration. With little time left and so much of life that she couldn't be part of anymore, she needed her art to feel that she was Tehuana Fridita, the Grand Dragon. About the year she spent in the hospital, Frida said, "I never lost my spirit. I always spent my time painting because they kept me going with Demerol [a narcotic painkiller], and this animated me and it made me feel happy."

By the end of the year she was able to work, lying on her back for four or five hours a day. She painted *My Family* in the hospital, a collective portrait of her grandparents, her parents on their wedding day, her older sisters as the middle-aged women they were, and Frida and Cristina as young women. Frida had painted her interior picture of them: her father is the handsome man she always loved and looked up to, her older sisters look motherly as they were to their little Frida, and Cristina, Frida's rival, is long-haired and pretty.

Through her work Frida transcended her deterioration. She was painting fewer self-portraits and less-violent images, but *Self-Portrait with Dr. Juan Farill,* painted in 1951 and depicting an older Frida, shows the same intensity as earlier works. With her living room as the background, Frida, dressed in a plain white smock and long black skirt, sits in a wheelchair. Her feet don't show, because the wheels have replaced them. Her blouse, resembling a hospital gown, is oversized, probably to hide a thick corset. Beside her is an easel with a completed painting of Dr. Juan Farill, Frida's most trusted physician in Mexico. Although her hair is gray at the temples and her face has aged, her hands possess her dual strengths of art and love. Frida holds paintbrushes dripping blood onto her white shirt, and her palette is covered by a heart larger than her head, the images signifying that she paints with her heart and blood. Farill's face, also larger than Frida's, possesses more life force than Frida's. He is like the saintly presence in a *retablo*, for it was he who relieved her pain. The idea of a heavenly spirit also suggests death. This is a portrait of a dying woman.

All her life Frida took pride in her beauty. She watched her weight constantly so as not to grow stout like her mother and sisters. Perhaps Frida stopped painting self-portraits because the mirror beside her bed revealed her deterioration: time, alcohol, drugs, and pain had changed her from a vibrant, magnetic woman into an often vacant, irritable invalid. Her face no longer comforted her, and while the rest of her body remained youthful, her lower back was a mass of scars. Of all life's losses, the loss of her beauty may have been the one that ultimately defeated her.

One of Frida's last portraits shows her with her hair down, lines in her face and neck, her eyes sunken and weary. At the bottom of the picture, as though it were a tombstone, Frida declares: "Here I have painted myself, Frida Kahlo, with the image from the mirror. I am 37 years old and it is the month of July in 1947. In Coyoacan, Mexico, the place where I was born.''

Frida clung to anything that gave her a reason to live, and children, who affirmed hope for the future, became especially important. Her last pupil, a nine-year-old Indian boy from Oaxaca named Vidal Nicolas, touched her affection for the young as well as linked her to the Indian culture of which she was so proud. Vidal traveled from his pueblo and unobtrusively spent hours watching Frida paint. Believing in his youth and heritage as well as his talent, Frida planned to send him to art school when he was older, though she didn't live long enough to fulfill that promise.

At the beginning of 1951, Frida left the hospital in less pain but barely able to walk. She made a bedroom for herself next to the studio upstairs, where she stayed most of the time. Only rarely did she enjoy singing around the dining-room table or strolling through the garden to pet her animals. Friends came to visit as always, but Frida spent more and more time alone. She had always treated her servants as family, but now they became her chief companions.

Frida's body may have been ready to rest, but not her spirit. When she came home from the hospital, she said there were three things she wanted to do: "Paint, paint, paint." In the mornings, when she was strongest, Frida painted in bed, or if she felt well enough, in her studio or outside on the patio. Friends came by in the after-noon, mostly women friends who didn't work, and Frida soaked up their tenderness in her weak, childlike state, welcoming substitute mothers and sisters to care for her. Cristina and Matilde visited almost every day.

When Frida was rested, friends took her out of the house to see the life she cherished, the ordinary people in pueblos and in the markets. Frida's nurse, Judith Ferreto, would reluctantly give Frida the double tequila she demanded, knowing the drink took the edge off her pain and gave her a temporary boost to stand and talk with *la gente*. Although Frida had traveled far from her Preparatoria days, she had never lost the feeling that she was, in spirit, a street urchin.

By 1952 Frida's painting style had changed to looser, sometimes messy strokes. Some of her late work is so frantic that only her signature identifies it as hers. Alcohol and painkillers contributed to this, and so did her haste to make pictures for "dough," as Frida would say, imitating American gangster talk. Her hurry also came from knowing how little time she had left. Many of the paintings were still lifes of fruit, sensuous and vibrant as her early self-portraits. Watermelons cut open, juicy and round, roots surrounding the composition, recall the power of Frida's earlier works, but a new addition in many of the late paintings is a Mexican flag, often stuck into a piece of fruit, almost as an afterthought. This was as close as she would get to a political message. Communism gave her a link to Diego, and it gave her hope for the future of the world. Childless, she wanted a sense that her passions and beliefs would live on, so Stalin became her savior in a desperate effort to find a leader to fulfill her dreams.

At the end of 1952, Frida's shrinking life was brightened by the repainting of La Rosita, the *pulqueria* the Fridos had painted during the war. Because Diego's sixty-sixth birthday was on December 8, Frida arranged a Christmas party to celebrate the holiday, his birthday, and the second opening of the *pulqueria*. All afternoon crowds of friends moved from La Rosita to the Blue House, while Frida stayed home, visited with a few friends, and wistfully watched the fun. Late in the day Frida suddenly jumped up and ripped off her corset. Hair loose and flowing, her face full of the exhilaration of setting her body free, she shouted, "No more! Never again! Never again, no matter what happens! Never again!" And she walked out of the house, joined the party, and never wore a corset again.

Tree of Hope, Hold Steady shows graphically what the operations did to Frida. The left half of the picture shows her on a hospital gurney, her back dripping with blood from her latest surgical incision. Beside her sits a young and vibrant Tehuana Frida, dressed in red holding a brace and a little banner that says, *"Arbol de esperanza, Mantente Firme"* (Tree of hope, keep steady). Her presence is a comfort to her suffering companion. The strong Frida represents the part of her that gave her strength for thirty years to fight pain, fear of death, and betrayal by those she loved most. Expressed through her art, this spirit was her ultimate brace.

CHAPTER 13

La Pelona

FRIDA'S friends suffered as they watched her health decline, able to do little more than distract her temporarily from her fate. Lola Alvarez Bravo, longtime friend and photographer, felt special rapport with Frida not only as a fellow artist but also as a woman married to a famous artist. Her husband was Manuel Alvarez Bravo, Mexico's best-known photographer. Lola, an early enthusiast of Frida's painting, described her friend as "the only painter who gave birth to herself" through her art. But now she feared that *la pelona*, death, was closer to Frida than birth: "The struggle of the two Fridas was in her always, the struggle between one dead Frida and one Frida that was live. They had just performed a bone transplant, and unfortunately, the bone was diseased and they had to remove it again. I realized that Frida's death was quite near." Her right foot and spine were deteriorating quickly, and the doctors were unable to help.

Lola owned the Galeria Arte Contemporaneo in the Zona Rosa, a fashionable part of Mexico City. Ironically, in spite of all of Frida's recognition in Europe and the United States, she had never been given a solo exhibition in Mexico. Lola believed it was time because Frida deserved it, and because she thought, "Honors should be given to people while they are still alive to enjoy them, not when they are dead."

The moment Frida heard the news, she felt better, enjoying the sweetness of finally being appreciated at home. Fueled by anticipation, she designed invitations on brightly colored paper she made into little books bound with woolen yarn. Looking like the beautifully lettered notes she wrote to Alejandro when she was young, and with a spirit characteristic of her writing, Frida composed and hand-wrote the invitations: "With friendship and love, people of the heart, I have the pleasure of inviting you to my humble exhibition. At eight o'clock—after all, you have a clock—I wait for you in the Galeria of this Lola Alvarez Bravo. You will find Amberes 12 and with open doors to the street; with luck you will not get lost, because that is the end of the details. I only want you to tell me your good and honest opinion. You have read and written, you have the highest knowledge. These paintings I painted with my own hands, they wait on the walls for my brothers and sisters to like them. Good, my dear friend, with true friendship, I thank you from my soul. Frida Kahlo de Rivera."

Her brief rally into health was soon followed by a turn for the worse. The day before the show, April 13, 1953, Frida's doctors told her not to leave her bed, let alone attend the grand fiesta her show was certain to become.

But only *la pelona* could stop Frida. Between drugs and pain she might have looked frightening, and she might have put her life in danger, but she was determined to attend her first and, most likely, last show. She sent her four-poster bed to the gallery, with instructions to place it where she could receive her guests, just as she did at home. The bed was placed in the center of the room, so that Frida would be surrounded by her art.

The phone rang all day long at the gallery with everyone asking, "Would Frida be there?" everyone wanted to know. By seven o'clock hundreds had gathered outside, hoping to be admitted to the invitation-only opening. Lola Alvarez Bravo tried to keep people out until Frida arrived, because she thought that once the room was full, it would be very difficult for her to get in. But the crowd grew so restless, they opened the doors.

As the room filled with noise and people, a siren could be heard above the din. Frida had arrived by ambulance with a police escort and made her entrance on a hospital stretcher. Bravo said, "The photographers and reporters were so surprised that they were almost in shock. They abandoned their cameras on the floor. They were incapable of taking any pictures of the event." One of the few photographs taken that night shows Frida greeting guests whose faces betray their alarm at seeing her so diminished, despite her effort to appear vivacious. Guillermo Monroy remembered, "Frida was very fixed up, but tired and sick."

Dressed in Tehuana clothes, Frida entertained in her bed with its mirror under the canopy, the small Judas figures dangling over her, and photographs of friends, family, and Communist leaders taped to the headboard. One of her paintings hung from the footboard. Like Frida and all that surrounded her, her bed suggested daring, style, childlike tastes, and warmth.

The room was filled with energy, all of it focused on Frida, who drew it in like oxygen. People lined up to greet her, pay her homage, but there was also a feeling they were saying good-bye. Frida talked, told jokes, sang, and drank until she could do no more. Any talk of sparing Frida's strength was out of the question; both Frida and Diego were enjoying their historical, cultural, and artistic place too much that night to end the evening voluntarily. It was like theater, and no one, especially the leading lady, cared if the performance seemed strained and slightly grotesque.

The exhibition lasted a month and received attention in Europe and the United States. Diego, Frida's friend and mentor, felt paternal pride when he described the show as "the most thrilling event of 1953. Anyone who attended it could not but marvel at her great talent. Even I was impressed when I saw all her work together."

In August, Frida went back to the hospital when her right leg became infected with gangrene. With Diego and Frida's old friend, Adelina Zendya present, Dr. Farill examined her crippled and twisted leg from which two toes had already been amputated. The doctor said, "You know, Frida, I think it is useless to just cut your toe, because of the gangrene. I think that the moment has come when it would be better to cut off your leg." Frida howled with anguish.

Diego burst into tears and muttered, "She is going to die, this is going to kill her."

Frida asked Adelina what she should do. With all eyes on her, Adelina first looked at the shrunken, degenerated foot and then at Frida's frightened face. "Well,

Frida," Adelina began, "you always used to call yourself 'Frida the gimp, with the peg leg.' So you will be lame. Now you are lame with much suffering. Your leg does not allow you to walk, and now there are very good artificial legs, and you are a person who knows how to overcome this kind of thing very well. Probably you will be able to walk and move more normally than with this leg that no longer is much use to you and that also gives you so many pains and makes you an invalid. And the sickness won't spread. So you no longer have to be 'Frida the gimp.' Think about it. Why don't you let them operate on you?"

Farill was grateful for Adelina's advice, after which Frida turned to him and asked to be prepared for the operation. Despite the terror of the amputation, Frida still couldn't bear people pitying her, and she donned her bravest face. On the night before the operation, she played with a little clay deer and monkey Adelina had sent her. Friends who came to visit found Frida dressed up, ready to cheer them up. "But what's the matter? Look at your faces, it's as if there were a tragedy! What tragedy? They are going to cut off my *pata* [paw]. So what?" Whether the dress and the words were for her friends or herself, no one could know, but at the least her cheerful and beautiful facade distracted everyone, including herself.

But those closest to Frida—her nurse, Judith; Adelina; and Diego—knew that she saw the amputation as the beginning of her complete disintegration. After the visitors left her that night, the room became quiet with fear and despair. Frida let go of the tree of hope and declared, "Night is falling in my life." After the operation, which removed her right leg at the knee, Frida refused to talk,

walk, see anyone, or paint. When Judith tried to coax
her into feeling anything, even rage, a psychiatrist told
her to stop, because he believed Frida didn't want to live
anymore.

In her art Frida shocked people by revealing her broken heart or her broken spine, but in life she didn't want
to expose her physical pain and have to endure pity. The
amputation had left her vulnerable: she could no longer
control what people knew about her. She was missing
a part of herself, and for a woman who reveled in her
physical presence to charm, persuade, and prevail, the
amputation was not a lifesaving measure but a slow
murder.

"Without her leg it was impossible to help her anymore," Judith said. "The operation destroyed a personality. She loved life, she really loved life, but it was
completely different after they amputated her leg."
Despite Frida's despair, her will to live emerged from
time to time. After three months her natural coordina-
tion and grace helped her learn to walk with a false leg.
Long skirts and the red leather boots she had especially
made hid the fact that she didn't have both feet. The
shoes had little bells on them, and Frida said she would
"dance her joy" in them.

By the spring of 1954, Frida felt ready to paint again,
and she often did so in bed after breakfast. If she felt
well enough, she worked in the studio in her wheelchair, with a sash around her middle and the back of
the chair to give the support she needed without a corset. One of her last paintings, and one of her most beautiful, is a still life of round watermelons, some cut, some
whole. On the melon closest to the viewer, just waiting
to be bitten into, Frida wrote: *"Viva La Vida"* (Long live

life). No matter how restricted and difficult her life had become, she hadn't lost her passion for all that was alive.

Frida moved her bed into the hallway between her studio and bedroom, because its large picture window looked out onto her garden. She watched the colors of the day change, followed a bird's flight, listened to the rain. Maybe she remembered the lifetime of rich pleasures she had enjoyed among the plants, pets, and friends in that courtyard. She no longer wanted visitors; only Cristina and Judith stayed close to her. Diego tried to comfort Frida, but often he stayed away, perhaps unable to bear seeing her so changed.

The amputation had eased some of her pain, but her spine still caused tremendous suffering. Frida escaped it through painkillers and alcohol, but she paid a price. One day Frida called Judith, crying and begging her to come over. Judith found Frida in the studio, her hands smeared with paint, brushes dripping onto the floor. Her hair was uncombed, and her dress was spattered with paint. Frida had always been meticulous about her appearance, her house, her finances, but most of all about her work tools. Judith understood Frida's shame and frustration. She asked her if she wanted help, and Frida gratefully accepted. "Which dress do you want to wear?" Judith asked.

"Please bring me the one you prepared before you left, because all those things were done with love, and there is no love around here now. And you know that love is the only reason for living. So bring the one that was made with love." Judith washed and dressed her, fixed her hair, and put her to bed.

Frida longed to be in the world, especially at Diego's side, but it was too late. She made one final attempt, on a cold rainy day, July 2, 1954, when she left her bed to march in a wheelchair pushed by Diego in a Communist demonstration protesting U.S. interference in Guatemala. The C.I.A. had replaced the liberal government of President Jacobo Arbenz with the right-wing rule of General Castillo Armas. Frida, an example of fortitude to the ten thousand who marched from Santo Domingo Plaza to the Zocalo, told newspaper reporters, "In spite of my sickness I came to lend my support to this movement of solidarity of Mexicans with Guatemalans. Guatemala's cause may be Mexico's cause tomorrow." Holding a placard bearing a peace dove, Frida, in a large wrinkled kerchief covering her hair, looked weary and sick. The march was her last public appearance. She withstood the bone-chilling weather for four hours and returned home with pneumonia. Trying to prepare for death, she thought about how it would feel to be lowered into the ground on her back, and having spent so much time in hospitals and at home in this position, she asked to be cremated.

Frida willed herself to live for one more fiesta on July 7, to celebrate her forty-seventh birthday. She asked a friend, Teresa Proenza, to sleep over: "I want, as a present, for you to stay here to accompany me so that you wake up here tomorrow." The morning began with friends singing "Las Mananitas," Mexico's birthday song. Later in the day, wearing makeup and a white dress, Frida entertained over one hundred friends in the dining room with a lunch of mole, chilis, and tamales. As usual she succeeded in getting everyone to enjoy the moment; death seemed far away as friends delighted in a last taste of an enchanting, beautiful, and vibrant Frida.

A few days later she wrote in her diary, "I hope the exit is joyful—and I hope never to come back—Frida."

On the night of July 12, Diego saw that Frida was gravely ill. He recalled, "When I went into her room to look at her, her face was tranquil and seemed more beautiful than ever. The night before she had given me a ring she had bought as a gift for our twenty-fifth anniversary, still weeks away. I asked her why she was presenting it so early and she replied, 'Because I feel I am going to leave you very soon.'"

Despite warnings from the doctor that Frida was very ill, Diego left to spend the night in San Angel. Frida awakened at four A.M. in terrible pain. Her nurse calmed her, and she went back to sleep. At six A.M. the nurse found Frida with her eyes open but not seeing, her hands icy cold. The nurse called for Manuel, Guillermo Kahlo's old driver, who had known Frida all her life, and he went to San Angel to tell Diego, *"Murio la nina Frida"* (the little girl, Frida, died).

Friends immediately filled the Blue House. They dressed Frida in a black skirt and white Indian blouse, braided her hair, and adorned her with rings, earrings, and necklaces. Flowers and dolls surrounded her bed. All day long friends came by tearfully to see Frida. Diego, who seemed to have become an old man overnight, had locked himself in his room downstairs, not wanting to see or talk to anyone.

Andreas Iduarte, director of the Palace of Fine Arts and Frida's fellow Cachucha, gave permission to allow Frida's coffin to lie in state in the Palace overnight through the next morning as an honor befitting a national idol. This was a courageous decision on Iduarte's part, since the Mexican government was anti-Communist. Diego, Frida's sisters, and close friends Lola Alvarez Bravo and Juan O'Gorman stood guard over the body. Iduarte cautioned Diego not to make the ceremony political, and Diego agreed, but when Arturo Bustos suddenly covered the coffin with a huge red flag emblazoned with a hammer and sickle, Diego refused to remove it.

Had Frida been alive, she may have found all this passion about politics amusing. While Communist friends believed Frida was a loyal party member, others were certain her commitment to Communism was really nothing more than an embrace of Diego. The flag cost Iduarte his job, and Diego was readmitted into the Communist party two and a half months later.

If Surrealism ever fit Frida, it applied to her funeral. Despite the rain hundreds of people crowded inside and outside the building where the cremation took place. Frida's coffin was open, showing red carnations around her head and a *rebozo* over her shoulders. After friends read speeches and poems and shared memories about her, Frida was taken out of the coffin by Diego and the family and placed onto a rolling cart, which would take her into the oven. Diego kissed Frida on the forehead, and everyone sang the song Frida had long ago whistled to Diego, the Communist "Internationale."

As the oven door opened, Frida's body moved slowly toward the fire as her friends sang songs of farewell. Stopping only when they felt the overwhelming heat of the fire, people cried and tried to take the rings off her fingers, just to keep something that belonged to her. As the cart hit the most intense heat, Frida's body suddenly sat up with blazing hair surrounding her face, looking, according to one witness, as though she were smiling in the center of a huge sunflower. She had left the world with a stunning image no one would ever forget.

In *Fruit of Life*, painted in 1953, a smiling orange sun reaches its warm veinlike rays out to the bananas, watermelons, and sunlike oranges below it. The rays also touch a white dove and the moon. On the bottom right Frida wrote "*Luz* [light]. Frida Kahlo." Out of her darkness she struggled to find and create life's light. Like the sun in her painting, Frida Kahlo spread her powerful rays and, through her character and art, touched the world.

Chronology

1907   Born on July 6, in Coyoacan, Mexico.

1910   Beginning of the Mexican Revolution. A decade of turmoil ensues in Mexico.

1922   Enters the National Preparatory School in Mexico City and becomes friends with Las Cachuchas, a nine-member club with only two girls. Becomes girlfriend of Alejandro Gomez Arias, later distinguished as one of Mexico's intellectual leaders. Meets Diego Rivera who is painting a mural at the school.

1925   Survives a near-fatal accident when the bus on which she and Alejandro are passengers is hit by a trolley. The accident leaves her with permanent injury and pain.

1926   Begins to paint during her long period of recovery.

1928   Shows her work to Diego Rivera who is impressed and encourages her.

1929   Marries Rivera on August 21. Begins to paint not only friends but the people of Mexico.

1930   Rivera commissioned to paint murals in San Francisco. Frida goes with him and meets Emmy Lou Packard and Dr. Leo Eloesser. Photographed by Imogen Cunningham.

1932   Has miscarriage in Detroit and suffers depression. Begins to paint on metal, in traditional *retablo* style. Begins to paint her life. Her mother dies.

1933   Nelson Rockefeller commissions Rivera to paint a mural in Rockefeller Center. A political dispute between the men leads to cancellation of the mural.

1934   Frida and Diego move into their new home in San Angel.

1937   Leon Trotsky stays with Frida and Diego, while Frida begins working more seriously.

1938   Has her first solo show at the Julien Levy gallery in New York. Edward G. Robinson becomes her first serious collector, purchasing four works.

1939   Invited to Paris as a Mexican Surrealist and participates in a Mexican show. Louvre buys one of her paintings.

1940   Divorces Diego at his request. Trotsky is assassinated at the orders of Stalin. Remarries Diego in San Francisco on December 8.

1943   Becomes a teacher of Los Fridos, her students, and they paint a *pulqueria* (bar) in Coyoacan.

1950   Hospitalized for one year during which time she paints lying in bed.

1953   Her first and only solo show in Mexico is held at the Lola Alvarez Bravo Gallery in Mexico City. Leg is amputated on July 27.

1954   Makes her last public appearance at a political rally. Develops pneumonia soon afterward and dies on July 13 in the same house in which she was born.

THE PAINTINGS OF FRIDA KAHLO

Much of Frida Kahlo's work exists today in private collections. Here is a sampling of paintings that are accessible for public viewing.

Frida and Diego Rivera, 1931. Oil on canvas, 39 × 31½". San Francisco Museum of Modern Art, Albert M. Bender Collection.

Portrait of Dr. Leo Eloesser, 1931. Oil on cardboard, 33½ × 23½". Collection University of California, San Francisco, School of Medicine.

My Dress Hangs There, 1933. Oil and collage on masonite, 18 × 19¾". Estate of Dr. Leo Eloesser, Hoover Gallery, San Francisco.

My Grandparents, My Parents, and I, 1936. Oil and tempera on metal panel, 12⅛ × 13⅝". The Museum of Modern Art, New York.

The Two Fridas, 1939. Oil on canvas, 67 × 67". Collection of the Museo de Arte Moderno, Mexico City.

Self-Portrait, 1940. Oil on masonite, 23½ × 15¾". Estate of Dr. Leo Eloesser, Hoover Gallery, San Francisco.

Self-Portrait, 1940. Oil on masonite, 23½ × 15¾". Estate of Dr. Leo Eloesser, Hoover Gallery, San Francisco.

Self-Portrait with Cropped Hair, 1940. Oil on canvas, 15¾ × 11". The Museum of Modern Art, New York.

Portrait of Don Guillermo Kahlo, 1952. Oil on canvas, 0.62 × 0.48 mts. The Frida Kahlo Museum, Mexico City.

Viva La Vida, 1954. Oil on masonite. 23⅓ × 20". The Frida Kahlo Museum, Mexico City.

Marxism Will Give Health to the Sick, 1954. Oil on masonite, 30 × 24". The Frida Kahlo Museum, Mexico City.

BIBLIOGRAPHY

"Bomb Beribboned." *Time* (November 1938): 29.

CHESSHER, MELISSA. "The Cult of Kahlo." *American Way 23* (December 1990): 62–68, 94–99.

CROMMIE, KAREN AND DAVID. *The Life and Death of Frida Kahlo.* San Francisco, California: The Serious Business Company, 1965. Film.

"Frida vs. Diego." *Art Digest 14* (November 1939): 8.

GRIMBERG, SALOMON. *Frida Kahlo: Das Gesamtwerk.* Frankfurt am Main: Verlag Neue Kritik, 1988.

GUTIERREZ, MARCO ANTONIO. "The Intense Duality of Frida Kahlo." *People's World 40* (November 1977): 10.

HELM, MACKINLEY. *Modern Mexican Painters.* New York: Harper & Row, 1941.

HERRERA, HAYDEN. *Frida: A Biography of Frida Kahlo.* New York: Harper & Row, 1983.

———. "Why Frida Kahlo Speaks to the 90's." *The New York Times* (October 28, 1990): Section II, page 1.

JENKINS, NICHOLAS. "Calla Lillies and Kahlos." *Artnews 90* (March 1991): 104–105.

KAHLO, FRIDA. Letters. Bertram Wolfe Archives, Hoover Institution, Stanford University, California.

KOZLOFF, JOYCE. "Frida Kahlo." *Women's Studies 6* (1978): 43–59.

The Meadows Museum. *Frida Kahlo.* Exhibition catalogue. Southern Methodist University, Dallas, Texas, 1989. Essay by Salomon Grimberg.

NEWMAN, MICHAEL. "The Ribbon Around the Bomb." *Art in America 71* (April 1983): 160–169.

Plaza de la Raza. *Frida Kahlo.* Catalogue. Los Angeles, 1987.

ROSE, BARBARA. "Chicana As Heroine." *Vogue 173* (April 1983): 152–154.

WOLFE BERTRAM D. *Diego Rivera: His Life and Times.* New York and London: Knopf, 1939.

WOLFE, BERTRAM D. *The Fabulous Life of Diego Rivera.* New York: Stein & Day, 1963.

ZAMORA, MARTHA. *Frida Kahlo: The Brush of Anguish.* San Francisco: Chronicle Books, 1990.

Index